Praise for
Sherry Stewart Deutschmann
and
Lunch with Lucy

"What Sherry Deutschmann has done in institutionalizing and sharing her employee-first philosophy shows that valuing workers first as people makes extraordinary business sense. By placing empathy and equal opportunity at the center of the business, you engage everyone in serving the customer. By paying a living wage and sharing profits equally, you unshackle workers from the tyranny of overtime and multiple jobs so they can focus on work and tend to their families. And by making yourself, as the leader, accessible to everyone, you gain important insight on your operations and your people. *Lunch with Lucy* is a refreshing must-read for leaders of companies of all sizes and levels of maturity."

—BETH BROOKE-MARCINIAK, Board Director eHealth and SHEEX, Former Global Vice Chair, Public Policy, EY, and Diversity and Inclusiveness Sponsor, EY

"*Lunch with Lucy* is a beautiful reflection of the author—an authentic leader whose empathy for those she led and for her customers helped propel her business to remarkable success. Sherry's practical insights are food for every aspiring leader and CEO looking to make a difference. *Lunch with Lucy* is a full buffet of wisdom."

—DR. MICHAEL BURCHAM, Shore Capital Partners

"I was hooked from page one. Such a compelling story told in a way that seems so not only doable, but the right thing to do. If we had more leaders like Sherry, corporations would be better people. She helps you envision a world full of compassion, understanding, and kindness. This is an underdog story that leaves you feeling inspired, uplifted, and full of admiration for the grit and determination this woman has. More of this, please!"

—FRAN DUNAWAY, CEO/Cofounder, TomboyX.com, Seattle, WA

"I hate most books about company culture—in fact, I can't even read them. We all know culture is important. But too often these books treat it as if it's the ultimate goal—not the means to an end—focusing on silly perks that trivialize the conversation. But as a senior editor with *Inc.*, *Forbes*, and *The New York Times*, I've been following Sherry Deutschmann for years. I know she's different, both as a business owner and as an author. She actually connects the dots between treating employees well and maximizing profits. Wondering how to get employees to care about the business as if they were owners? This book is the blueprint. It's also a fun read."

—LOREN FELDMAN, Chief Content Officer, 21 Hats

"Wow! An inspiring, touching, funny story that helps you build a better business, strengthen your own character, and even save capitalism from itself. Sherry is a genius at solving problems, and she tells you all her secrets! This is a must-read, can't-miss, save-your-life, save-your-company book."

—U.S. CONGRESSMAN JIM COOPER, Tennessee's 5th
Congressional District

"Our obsession with maximizing profits at the expense of everything else on the planet has caused immeasurable harm. We need a new model of doing business, and with perfect timing, along comes Sherry Deutschmann with a model we can follow to maximize profits *and* take care of people. Read this book, follow it, and spread it widely. There is another way—and Sherry has proven it."

—VICKI SAUNDERS, CEO, SheEO, Toronto, Canada

"Working at LetterLogic was one of the greatest experiences in my life. Sherry showed how one person can really make life better for so many. Just imagine if more businesses operated like hers. Think of how far a living wage would go towards eradicating poverty . . . "

—PATRICK JOHNSON, President, ProGraphic South, Nashville, TN

"I have known Sherry for 25+ years—back before she started her own business and was working as a sales rep and crushing it! Sherry's fierce approach to life translated throughout her entrepreneurial journey as she grew her business, her people, and herself. In *Lunch with Lucy* Sherry weaves a powerful message through her storytelling. If you truly listen, it will show you a path less travelled and one that will reveal greater fulfillment for both you and your teams."

—ANDY BAILEY, CEO, Founder, and Head Coach, Petra Coach

"Every successful business owner I've met, either male or female, has usually built effective teams. How well they did that was based on their treatment of their employees and executives. Deutschmann's approach of putting her people first ultimately led to a healthy bottom line, but it also invested in the company's success. This is an important book for all business owners."

—MARSHA FIRESTONE, PhD. President and Founder, Women Presidents' Organization and Women Presidents' Educational Organization

"Sherry is a shining example of a CEO who fully embodies authentic leadership. Decades ago, using her business as a vehicle for change, Sherry blazed a trail for many of us by defining a corporate culture that placed employees first. Lunch with Lucy is an inspiring story and a gift to any entrepreneur who wants to make a difference with and in their business."

—PAMELA CHALOULT, CEO, Practical Feet Advisors, and Social Impact Leader

"Sherry's voice, ultimately, is unapologetic. It's a voice that business owners must learn to cultivate to accelerate toward the realization of their greatest ideas and contributions to the marketplace and our world."

—CARLA HARRIS, Vice Chairman, Wealth Management, Morgan Stanley

"Wittingly, Sherry uses lunch as the framework through which we might transform our relationship to traditional workplace hierarchies. Perhaps, we—as workaholic Americans—should start eating lunch together again?!"

—ESTHER MORALES, Consultant and Former Executive Director, National Women's Business Council (NWBC)

"Sherry Stewart Deutschmann is the boss every employee wants to work for and every entrepreneur should want to be. *Lunch With Lucy* is a smart, honest, funny, touching, and inspiring story about a woman who succeeded in business because of her own deeply held values—especially her commitment to her people. Whether you're an experienced leader or just starting out in business, you will find many practical and inspiring lessons in *Lunch With Lucy*. I've been a non-profit CEO for 30 years, and I lost count of the times I thought, "Damn! I wish I'd thought of that.""

—MARSHA BAILEY, Founder and CEO,
WEV (Women's Economic Ventures)

"Sherry's proven track record making the Inc. 5000 list 10 years in a row clearly demonstrates the powerful and profitable force of marrying heart-driven intention with thought-inspired action. Sherry made an immediate impact on EarthKind after I heard her story, and a lasting impact on me as a female entrepreneur who's out to change how pests are controlled—and ultimately how business is done. If more business functioned this way, we may no longer see 85% of workers hating their jobs, 38 million households living in poverty, or another 96 million close behind."

—KARI WARBERG BLOCK, Founder and CEO, EarthKind

"I have worked with literally hundreds of highly talented executives, but I have never met anyone who understands the transformative power of a simple conversation the way Sherry does. If you spend any time at all with Sherry, you come away changed—more motivated, more hopeful, and feeling like a better version of yourself. Her generosity of spirit just glows."

—MARY SOBON, Executive Coach, m2 Consulting

"Sherry is one of the smartest and most caring entrepreneurs I've ever met. She started and grew an uber-successful company, not only in size but in the impact she had on everyone who worked for her. She was a pioneer in what is known today as "conscious capitalism" and was playing the "Infinite Game" as Simon Sinek coined it in his latest book. Sherry treated everyone who worked for her—and every stakeholder in her company's ecosystem—as true partners and peers. She is a walking example of a servant leader, and her company's success is living proof of how treating your people like they should be treated can take a company to heights you never expected."

—RYAN TANSOM, Cofounder, Arkona

"Sherry's story is compelling and captivating. In my nearly 20 years teaching at Vanderbilt, she is the single most impactful and inspiring speaker—both for my students and myself—that I have hosted. Her grit, determination, and business savvy are only surpassed by her care and commitment to her people and community. The world would be a better place if we would all read and implement her leadership characteristics. *Lunch with Lucy* is a must-read!"

—KRISTEN TOMPKINS, HOD Lecturer and Director of Capstone, Vanderbilt University

"Creating a healthy culture within an organization is not only good for retention, but it's good for business. Sherry Deutschmann's employee-first leadership style created brand advocates that propelled LetterLogic forward. This book is a fascinating story of how she did that, but it is also an actionable field guide for entrepreneurs looking to follow in her footsteps. So pull up a chair and dig in."

—JACQUELINE HAYES, MBA, NAWBO Board Member, Chief Marketing Strategist + Principal, Crayons & Marketers

"Sherry Deutschmann pioneered past complacent competition to drive a culture of empathy that not only engaged her employees' hands *and* hearts, but she set up a winning recipe for a successful exit. A must-read for any entrepreneur looking to maximize their impact!"

—ERIC S. DEEMS, HealthTech Entrepreneur and Real Estate Investor

LUNCH
with LUCY

Maximize Profits
by Investing
in Your
People

LUNCH
with LUCY

Sherry Stewart Deutschmann

AN INC.
ORIGINAL

An Inc. Original
New York, New York
www.anincoriginal.com

This work is being published under the An Inc. Original imprint by an exclusive arrangement with *Inc.* Magazine. *Inc.* Magazine and the Inc. logo are registered trademarks of Mansueto Ventures, LLC. The An Inc. Original logo is a wholly owned trademark of Mansueto Ventures, LLC.

Distributed by Greenleaf Book Group

For ordering information or special discounts for bulk purchases, please contact Greenleaf Book Group at PO Box 91869, Austin, TX 78709, 512.891.6100.

Design and composition by Greenleaf Book Group
Cover design by Greenleaf Book Group

Publisher's Cataloging-in-Publication data is available.

Print ISBN: 978-1-7334781-0-6

eBook ISBN: 978-1-7334781-1-3

Part of the Tree Neutral® program, which offsets the number of trees consumed in the production and printing of this book by taking proactive steps, such as planting trees in direct proportion to the number of trees used: www.treeneutral.com

Printed in the United States of America on acid-free paper

20 21 22 23 24 25   10 9 8 7 6 5 4 3 2 1

First Edition

Lunch with Lucy is dedicated to the women and men of LetterLogic,
who worked alongside me to build our strong company.

I love you.

TAMMI Merchant	NIKKO Lloyd	MITCH Willman
MATT Motsinger	JENNIFER Anderson	GREG Brinkley
CARRIE Arkle	CORY Hutcheson	FREDDIE Brooks
ELIZABETH Geist	FRANK P. LaVarre	ANDREW Bustos
CHARLOTTE Hutson	HARVEY McClendon	MARIA Garcia
CARRIE Sublett	COLIN Griffin	TONYA Hawkins
LINCOLN Atwood	SCOTT Hunt	SIMONE Johns
MICHAEL Golden	DARIUS Banks	FRANKLIN Johnson
WEI Le	MERILIN Gonzalez	TAHEIM Washington
MICHAEL McDonald	TAKEETA Dale	JUSTIN Wilson
WILL Golden	RYAN Flood	AARON Lego
PATRICIA Vinson	MICHAEL Andrews	BRAD Stevens
DARIUS Norman	JAKSA Antic	GALEN Bultje
JASON DeMoss	BRENDA Berger	CHASE Drake
NANCY Fourre	KIMBERLY Childs	DAN Flanigan
AMANDA Flickinger	IAN McKinney	SAMANTHA Harris
DAVA Frierson	KHOUNMY Phinith	BRANDON Jones
DEMARCO Gurley	PAUL Profitt	ROSETTA McHenry
PATRICK Johnson	REGINALD Shye	KEONDRIA McHenry
SHERRY Hale	TANEKA Smith	MICHAEL Rose
ANDREW Kelley	MICHAEL Thackxton	AUSTIN Smith
CYNTHIA Milliken	PENNY Terry	JORDAN Smith
KYLE Levering	GORICA Zivak	DEREK Broadwater
MARTIN Majors	ERIC Hollingsworth	TARA Martin
CARLOS Mella	DAWN Lumley	HEATHER Oller
ROBB Pring	ERIN Boulware	CARL Motsinger
DEEJAY Washington	LAWSON Freeman	BRIAN Rawlings
DARLENE Washington	SUSIE Gilmer	BLAKE Moody
DAJOUR Williams	TRAVIS Lanier	JEREMY Burns
DANIEL Harris	NICK Manners	MATT Brinkley
MIKE Dills	KYLE Marcum	CHRISTIAN Maddox
HANNAH Dills	JACOB Schnittjer	PIERRE Gadea
KENNON Askew	PATRICK Scruggs	ARLEEN Kohn
	BRANDON Swift	

"There's more hunger for

love and appreciation in this world

than for bread."

–Mother Teresa

THE MENU

Last Course: *Dessert*

Acknowledgments

I can't believe I finally finished this book. It was a labor of love that took years to complete. Years! I'm sure there were times when my friends and family thought it was never going to end. Me too! Thanks to you all for not rolling your eyes every time I gave you an update.

Mark Deutschmann, my husband, is my biggest fan and fiercest competitor. When I started writing my book, he started writing his own. He won—having published his *One Mile Radius* in 2017. Mark, I love you with all my heart, but I'm still going to try to sell more books than you did. And to win every Scrabble game!

I happily entrusted the early pivotal editing of my book to Brooke White, and I'm forever grateful to her for her work. Brooke, thank you for your brilliant ideas and subtle prodding.

Thank you to the great team at Greenleaf Book Group. From Sally Garland, a patient, kind, thoughtful editor, to Chase Quarterman, the artist who created the beautiful cover, to Sam Alexander, brand strategist extraordinaire, and Jen Glynn, the project manager who kept everything on track—it was simply a joy to work with you all.

Thanks to Michael Brody-Waite and Michael Burcham for loving me enough to make me go back to the writing desk after the first iteration of this book. Guys, please, will you destroy the earlier version today?

Thank you to the women and men of LetterLogic. We built something great together. I will love you always.

To Eric Hollingsworth, Dava Frierson, Daniel Harris, Brenda Berger, and Jason DeMoss: You are unsung heroes in the LetterLogic story, powerhouses of work ethic and steadiness. I'm so glad I got to work alongside you.

Thank you to Scott Gray and Candy Jennings for making my life so much easier. You make it possible for me to do what I do. You are both magicians!

Thank you to Lucius Burch for giving me a chance by investing in LetterLogic in the early years. What a giant leap of faith you took, taking on such an unorthodox leader. I'm forever humbled and honored to be one of dozens of entrepreneurs who owe their success to you.

Whitney, thank you for giving me the greatest gifts I've ever received, my granddaughters Nikko and Reagan. I thought about you and them while writing this book. I love you all.

Mise en Place
(Everything in Its Place)

"Dessert is probably the most important stage of the meal, since it will be the last thing your guests remember before they pass out all over the table."

–William Powell

When you sit down for a meal, most people don't expect to eat dessert first. And when you sit down with a book, you don't expect to know the ending before you start reading. But I'm beginning this book with an unconventional approach: I'm sharing the ending before I give you all the juicy details of the story. Why? Because my approach to business is so unorthodox, so counter to what you learned in business school, that you might be tempted to dismiss it, unless you knew that my business was very successful. It was successful—not *in spite* of my unusual, empathetic leadership—but *because* of it.

Here are the CliffsNotes. I was a forty-two-year-old single mom with a high school education and meager savings when I cashed in my 401(k) and took a risk. I sold my personal belongings in a yard sale that yielded just enough cash to start a company—LetterLogic—in my basement, which defied every single rule of what makes a sure bet in business.

That business grew, debt-free, to a $40 million enterprise.

Inc. magazine recognized us as an Inc. 5000 company (one of the fastest-growing privately held businesses in the United States) for ten consecutive years. And along the way, we won national and international accolades, awards, and honors for one reason: our culture.

WHAT WAS SO SPECIAL ABOUT OUR CULTURE?

Our secret sauce had one key ingredient; one differentiator that made it possible for our little company to become the industry price leader with a Net Promoter score of 97. That one element was empathy. Yes, empathy.

> "Our culture of empathy was the direct result of leadership through empathy."

When people talk or write about LetterLogic's success, they often focus on the unusually generous benefits package: the 10 percent profit share distributed monthly, the fair living wages, the bring-your-kids-to-work perk, the monthly open-book financial meetings, the gift toward the purchase of a home. All of that is true. But those benefits were just the expression, the outcome, the effect of a culture of empathy; a culture where we truly cared for each other as if we were family. How did this culture come to be? Our culture of empathy was the direct result of leadership through empathy.

"But wait. Does the world need another book about business culture and leadership?" you might ask. "There are hundreds already!"

Yes, I believe the world does need just one more—this one—because this book promotes a business model that contradicts today's prevalent "customer-always-comes-first" strategy.

CUSTOMERS DON'T COME FIRST. EMPLOYEES DO

This book is about how we, the fifty employees of LetterLogic, built a very successful business by putting the needs of our employees, of *each other*, above the needs and interests of the customer—and the shareholder. It's about how we met with prospective customers and told them, to their faces, that we did not believe they came first. And after they picked their jaws up off the floor, our customers listened with rapt attention as we explained our philosophy. Our practice of taking great care of our employees created a team of happy people working together to take great care of the customers. The customers got it. In fact, they loved it. Once they got a taste of how our empathetic culture affected them, they became fiercely loyal to us. They became our greatest fans and advocates.

BUT HOW ABOUT YOUR COMPANY?

Is your culture healthy and are your employees happy, dedicated, and engaged? Don't be too sure. Have you read the 2018 Gallup poll on employee engagement? Its findings are shocking: Among US companies, 53 percent of all employees are "not engaged,"[1] which means they're clocking in and clocking out and doing the bare minimum necessary to collect a paycheck. They hate their jobs. Even worse, about 13 percent of them are "actively disengaged" and trying to influence their coworkers to be just as discontent as they are. This segment of your workforce can be so effective in their undermining efforts that Gallup concludes more than half of your employees—including those who are "engaged"—are actively looking for a new job (even as you sit here reading my words).

I didn't have access to the Gallup study before I started LetterLogic, but

---

1   Harter, Jim, "Employee Engagement on the Rise in the US," *Economy*, August 26, 2018, https://news.gallup.com/poll/241649/employee-engagement-rise.aspx

I didn't need it. I had been a stellar employee and dedicated to the company; but unfortunately, I wasn't being heard and I wasn't being valued. I became unhappy all on my own. And the unhappiness grew until I was "disengaged." I lived through the cycles of being engaged, disengaged, *actively* disengaged, and beyond.

The experience of being underappreciated and undervalued by my boss, despite my passion for his company and his customers, deeply influenced me and my actions. I wondered, *Did other employees feel the way I did? Did they have enthusiasm and passion for their jobs when they were first hired? Had they slowly lost that enthusiasm and passion?* Around the time I realized that I was losing faith in my boss, I read Kevin and Jackie Freiberg's book, *Nuts*. It's the story of how Herb Kelleher started Southwest Airlines based on the belief that happy flight attendants would create happy, loyal passengers. I was inspired. It made so much sense. The premise was simple.

When you put the needs of employees *first*, you create an environment that allows them to focus on the job at hand and ensures they are committed to your company's success. They will care as much as you do. When this happens, they will wow your customers with high-quality products and jaw-dropping service, and your customers will be willing to pay a premium for that. And, happy, loyal customers who pay a premium for your goods and services will deliver satisfying rewards to your shareholders. Everybody wins!

Lunch with Lucy is not a step-by-step book on how to get rich and build your company for a quick sale. It's about the people of LetterLogic—our *family members*—and how they unselfishly, empathetically looked out for each other and what happened when they did. It's about how I grew as a leader, through some poor decisions and stumbles, but always with an empathetic leadership business model as my guide. Our story is filled with practical, uncommon, commonsense approaches that will ensure that your employees have a voice and are heard. A dynamic where everyone has a voice and everyone is heard translates into a winning culture, which in turn builds a strong foundation for a healthy company with a healthy bottom line. This stuff works, and you're about to find out why.

Oh, one last thing. Who is Lucy and why are you having lunch with her? Well, Lucy was my alter ego—the not-the-CEO everywoman, the just-another-employee—who reserved her Wednesdays for one-on-one lunches with the employees of LetterLogic. The employee chose the date, the restaurant, who else (if anyone) would be seated at the table, and the topic of conversation. The time I spent as Lucy with my work family over those lunches was the most important time of my workweek. What I discovered at those lunches was the key that unlocked the doors of their hopes and dreams, their personal challenges, and their ideas for improving our company. "Lunch with Lucy" gave me the insights that allowed me to be a better, more empathetic leader who could support the team that created one extraordinary company.

First Course

APPETIZERS

1

The Brown-Bag Days
My Story

"When I was writing *Kitchen Confidential* I was in my 40s—I had never paid rent on time, I was 10 years behind on my taxes, I had never owned my own furniture or a car."

–Anthony Bourdain

INGREDIENTS:

GRIT AND DETERMINATION,
WITH A HEAVY SPRINKLE OF DELUSION.

I was a naïve twenty-five-year-old, newly divorced mom when I made the rash decision to leave the mountains of North Carolina and move to Nashville to become a star. You might assume that anyone moving miles away from friends and family to pursue a singing career would have at least a few years of singing experience. I didn't. My experience was patchy at best: One of my friends at the time, a singer and guitarist, had a paying gig at Little Switzerland, a resort hotel in the Blue Ridge Mountains, and he let me sing a few duets and some solos; my brother Carl allowed me to sing a decent rendition of Linda Ronstadt's "Blue Bayou" at his wedding reception; and when our family friend John Moye, a gifted pianist, came to visit our house, I constantly begged, pleaded, and harassed him until he played—as I stood over his shoulder singing into his ear.

And there you have it—the complete unabridged accounting of my singing history. Definitely not enough to warrant a professional singing career, but I was determined, nonetheless.

Before taking the final leap, I had driven to Nashville to audition for the live TV show *You Can Be a Star*—a singing contest televised from Opryland, just behind the Grand Ole Opry. It was a precursor to *The Voice* and *American Idol,* but it was dedicated to country music.

The morning of the audition, the show's producer came out to speak to the dozens of waiting hopefuls and told us not to be discouraged if we didn't pass the audition. Even country legend Randy Travis had failed the same audition but still went on to become a huge star. Bolstered by that knowledge, I gave an adequate performance and passed the audition. A few weeks later, I drove back to Nashville to compete.

I selected Bonnie Raitt's song "Darlin'" for the competition. I walked out on stage wearing a new blue polyester dress with massive shoulder pads and a plunging neckline (it was the '80s), and I froze. The stage fright was crippling, and I delivered a sad, sorry version of the song I loved. After the scores were tabulated, I came in third place. Don't congratulate me. The show only had three contestants per episode! Coming in last should have been a clue to me that I wasn't cut out to be a singer, but I still thought I could be a star and was still determined to move to Nashville.

I'd like to be able to tell you that I had a stash of money saved just in case it took more than a few weeks to get a record deal. (If you know anything at all about the music business, that sentence alone proves how naïve and delusional I was.) Or, it would be good if I could say I had a great education or some other amazing skills I could have called upon to help me get a footing in my new town—or, if worst came to worst, that I had a few assets I could sell to pay the rent. But none of that was my reality.

This Was My Reality

- **MONEY:** After I paid my first month's rent, I had less than $200 to my name.

- **EDUCATION:** I had a diploma from Avery County High School, Newland, North Carolina.

- **SKILLS:** Well, I was then (and believe I still am) the best toilet scrubber in the South. My sisters and I cleaned houses for the wealthy families who had vacation homes in our ski-resort town. And I helped my sister Connie clean gas station restrooms for $5 a stall.

- **SUPPORT SYSTEM:** Yes, I had that—an adorable three-year-old daughter, Whitney Meghan Lloyd, who gave me lots of love and encouragement. We didn't know a soul in Nashville, but we had each other, and we'd make it together.

- **ASSETS:** Something of value I could sell if times got tough? Well yes, I had one. It was Jezzy (short for Jezebel), a sort-of-white, diesel, 1976 Volkswagen Rabbit with over 200,000 miles on her. Jezzy had belonged to my father's construction company. Their mechanic used her primarily to visit various job sites to maintain the backhoes and earthmovers and other heavy equipment. Once parked too close to the edge of a cliff, she had taken a tumble off a construction site on Beech Mountain. Though still functional, she was lopsided and dented all over, with her white paint quickly becoming rust-colored. The steering wheel and blue vinyl interior were caked with black grease and mud when I bought her for the bargain price of $1. Yes, one hundred pennies. (Later, you'll find out why many thought I was ripped off!)

Though Jezzy was definitely the ugliest car on the road, she had one great feature: a Blaupunkt stereo system with multiple speakers, sub-woofers, and a cassette player. Just days before my move to Nashville, the stereo and speakers were stolen. My one and only asset suddenly lost about 95 percent of her value. But I left for Nashville anyway and arrived in style.

SCRAPING BY

I moved to Nashville just as the now world-renowned Bluebird Cafe opened. It was, and still is, my "church"—my favorite room in the world. What an experience it was to sit in such a small venue and hear Grammy-award winning songwriters play and sing the songs they'd written.

This is the place in my story where I should have a tale of heartbreak and humiliation—where I sang at an open-mic night and someone crushed my dreams by telling me how awful I was. But, that's not what happened. Though I came in third and last place on *You Can Be a Star*, I was a solidly mediocre singer. Not awful. Not good. Just mediocre. A few nights at the Bluebird were all I needed to objectively gauge my talent and realize I didn't have the goods. While I secretly harbored a ridiculous dream of being discovered, I put my energy into making a living outside the music business.

Ironically, it was a combination of Jezzy and my religious background that led to my being hired for my first job in Nashville. I was raised in a Jehovah's Witness household, and it was expected that all members of the congregation participate in "field service," where we went door-to-door to share our faith. In my hometown of Banner Elk, North Carolina, the demographic swung wildly from the very poor to the very wealthy. In rural, mountainous, western North Carolina, there were homes with dirt floors and no indoor plumbing standing in stark contrast to impressive chalets owned by celebrities and wealthy southerners. My earliest recollection of knocking on a stranger's door, introducing myself, and delivering a brief presentation was as a third grader, age nine.

Whether the floors were dirt or heated slate, Jehovah's Witnesses approached every household. Field service taught me to talk to people of all socioeconomic levels, and I learned to adjust my message to fit the setting and circumstance. I grew confident speaking to strangers and developed empathy and compassion for those who were less fortunate than I was. And I learned to handle rejection. As a third grader, I had no way of knowing what an asset that skill would turn out to be.

While I was looking for a "real" job in Nashville, I heard somewhere that car dealerships didn't require their salespeople to have college degrees or even

"I've been knocking on doors since I was eight or nine years old. I can definitely handle rejection!"

any previous selling experience. I also heard they provided a free "demo" car to drive. Jezzy's dilapidated state inspired me to check into it. I drove her over to a Lincoln Mercury dealership, parked in front of the showroom, and went in to ask about a job.

After a short wait, I had a friendly conversation with the general manager who was encouraging. He said, "Your timing is good. We were just talking about adding a few women to the sales force. Tell me, what do you know about cars?"

"Nothing, really," I admitted.

He asked, "Well, what do you drive?"

I pointed out the showroom window to my Jezebel. "That."

The look on his face was a mixture of horror and disgust and incredulity.

After a lengthy silence, he said, "Listen, young lady. The car business is really tough. Long hours. Lots of rejection. Can you handle rejection?"

I chuckled. "Yes, sir! I was raised as a Jehovah's Witness, and I've been knocking on doors since I was eight or nine years old. I can definitely handle rejection!"

He laughed out loud and exclaimed, "You're hired!" Then he lowered his voice and added, "On one condition: You gotta promise to never park that piece of shit car on our property again." I started working at the Lincoln-Mercury dealership a few days later, parking Jezzy just past the property line but still in sight of the showroom door.

New salespeople were required to sell six cars before they got a demo to drive. Whether out of pity or embarrassment, the general manager pulled me aside during my first week and told me to pick out a car. He also told me to get Jezzy out of sight for good. I paid $1 for her, and now I had to pay $150 to get rid of her—most of my first paycheck. Now you understand why some people think I was ripped off.

The car business was tough. I had a hard time making ends meet. In fact, too often, they just didn't. Every month, I had to make the choice between paying the electric bill or paying for childcare. Or food. Though it was humiliating at the time, I can now laugh about the time my mom and dad drove five hours over the mountains (unannounced) to visit Whitney and me. They couldn't call to tell me they were coming, because I didn't have a phone. This was before cell phones, and I didn't have a landline, so they just showed up. They were appalled that we were living without electricity and had been for several days.

I assured them we were all right and pointed to my cooler, filled with ice, milk, and a few essentials. We'd learned to take quick showers in cold water and to make do. When we needed clothes or household goods, we went to Goodwill or Southern Thrift. We didn't eat in restaurants. Such is the life of many single moms. Somehow, we just found a way.

And one more thing: Aside from the fact that I was barely scraping by selling cars and living paycheck to paycheck, I foolishly started dating my boss. I bet you can guess how that worked out. One of us had to leave. And it wasn't him.

TAKEAWAY BOX:

Seasons change . . . and dreams do too. Just as the door to one path closes, new doors are right there in front of you. Look ahead.

2

A Recipe for Disaster

"I'm not saying my wife is a bad cook, but she uses a smoke alarm for a timer."

–Bob Monkhouse

INGREDIENTS:

JUST THE RIGHT AMOUNT OF SIMMERING:
DON'T RUSH.

Over the next several years, I held other jobs that would inform the kind of leader I eventually became. They were all in sales, mostly for medical goods and services. Along the way, a headhunter convinced me to consider a sales opportunity with a printing company that had identified a new niche for hospitals.

My first reaction was: *There's no way I'd work for a printing company. How boring!* But, the headhunter insisted I talk to them. "I think you're right for this job, and I think you're going to like them."

Mostly just to get the headhunter off my back, I took the meeting. It was a traditional printing company that produced letterhead, business cards, and the like. They were planning a new division that involved printing and mailing patient billing statements for hospitals. They didn't have the equipment to do this type of printing. They didn't have the IT system in place to receive patient data electronically. They didn't have any marketing materials. And . . . they didn't even have a service agreement to use if they were able to convince a hospital to buy the service. What they *did* have was a brilliant vice president/information technology director they trusted to make it all happen.

> "I went from making so little money I couldn't keep the lights on to making six figures."

The headhunter's instincts were right. I liked them, and they liked me, and thus began my career in processing patient statements for the healthcare industry. It took about six months to sell my first account, but after that, almost everyone I presented to said yes. The division grew by leaps and bounds. I went from making so little money I couldn't keep the lights on to making six figures; from barely being able to pay the rent to owning a beautiful home and flipping houses as a hobby; from that gnarly old VW to a sleek black Jaguar.

FROM THE FRYING PAN INTO THE FIRE

During this time, I learned a crucial lesson in entrepreneurship: Growing too fast can kill a company. The company experienced exceptional growth early and fast, which put a great strain on our IT infrastructure. Our lone, brilliant IT guru worked around the clock. He often spent the night in his office to keep everything running. He was so busy adding new clients that he didn't have time to build a more scalable system; he only had time for band-aiding and duct-taping. The system he'd begun was not sustainable at our growth rate. His crazy schedule wasn't sustainable either. None of us should have been surprised when he left one night and never came back.

Losing our vice president of IT was disastrous for the business. Most of the code was in his head, and the team of IT professionals we brought in to replace him had a very hard time working with his system. Unable to service our clients properly, we started losing them. The IT team worked to build a new system while I continued to sell and add more customers to a broken system.

In addition to selling, I started pitching in to help other departments, doing whatever I could to keep us going. I worked in billing, production, and data mapping, and I hand-inserted thousands of letters into envelopes each night at home. But we continued to struggle, which put further pressure on the company owner and his family. Eventually, the strain was too much and the company was sold to a few local investors, one of whom became my new boss and our CEO. I was excited to have a clean slate with the new ownership team. I renewed my resolve and commitment to make the business successful.

> **"Whatever could possibly go wrong went wrong."**

On weekdays, I worked doggedly, selling services to new customers to build the top line. On nights and weekends, I cleaned the bathrooms, pulled weeds, and removed trash from the parking lot. I even laid the ceramic tile flooring for the IT department. But we continued to experience significant quality issues. In fact, things got worse. Much worse.

It seemed as if Murphy's Law had descended upon us. Whatever could possibly go wrong went wrong. I imagine you're thinking, *Heck, all you're doing is printing and mailing bills. How can you screw that up? What's the worst thing that could happen?* A lot!

Let me explain.

We printed and mailed the bills upside down. This meant they were "mailed" but didn't go anywhere because the address didn't appear in the envelope window. The result was that the patient never got the bill, which meant the hospital didn't get paid, and the patient's credit got dinged.

We mailed the bills late. Sometimes a week late, which meant that when patients received the bill, they had fewer days to make a payment before the next phase of the billing/collecting cycle began. For the hospital, even one extra day added to the revenue cycle has a negative impact on their financial health.

We printed and mailed the statements in triplicate. How is that a problem? Well, tell me, how would you feel about a business that sent you three copies of the same bill in one day? All in different envelopes? Aggravated? Angry? Doubtful of their competence? All of the above? All of the above.

Sometimes we didn't mail the statements at all, which meant the patient didn't get a bill and the debt was turned over to a collection agency.

Sometimes we printed the bills on the wrong paper, and sometimes we mailed your bill to someone else by accident.

We did all these things. Many times. Almost daily.

With all these problems, my role devolved into "professional apologizer," even though technically, by that time, I was vice president of sales. I became very good at groveling. My priority each day was to field calls from angry customers, try to explain what had happened, and what we were doing to make sure it didn't happen again. But it did happen again, and again, and again. It was like a mad combination of *Groundhog Day* and whack-a-mole. I don't recommend it.

"He simply lacked the empathy to see how our mistakes affected the lives of others."

As our problems mounted, with increasingly severe consequences, it became necessary to include the CEO in some of my crisis-management calls with clients. Though he was gracious and charming with them, he couldn't provide what they needed—the assurance that we were addressing and resolving our mistakes; that we wouldn't continue to make them. Oddly, while I was a nervous wreck before, during, and after these calls, my boss was seemingly unaffected. At first, I admired his stoicism—until I realized that wasn't what it was. He simply lacked the empathy to see how our mistakes affected the lives of others. He truly did not care.

I recall one conversation in particular with my favorite customer, someone who'd become my friend and mentor. The customer was on speakerphone as we tried to explain our most recent gaffe. She was losing patience with us. Her confidence had eroded, and she warned us that even one more mistake would force her to move her business elsewhere.

Though I had been expecting the news, it still hit me in the gut. She was our biggest customer and represented over 10 percent of our revenue. She was issuing a final warning to us. We ended the call, and there I was, with a heavy heart, full of worry that I was in danger of losing a friend and a large chunk of my income.

You might be wondering what my boss's reaction to the call was. He thrust his palm toward me for a celebratory high-five, his face sporting a big grin. I refused to return the high-five gesture, incredulous. What was he thinking? I suppose he was happy that she didn't yank the business then and there. But his lack of empathy for our customer and the havoc we'd wreaked on her business—and his lack of empathy *for me* and the potentially negative impact to my livelihood if she went elsewhere—was staggering. Not to mention demoralizing, disrespectful, arrogant, and counterproductive. Talk about a recipe for disaster.

TAKEAWAY BOX:

Growing too quickly without a strong, positive cultural foundation will give your business heartburn. And loss.

3

Setting My Own Table

"Never doubt that a small group of thoughtful, committed citizens can change the world; indeed, it's the only thing that ever has."

–Margaret Mead

INGREDIENTS:

DOGGED OPTIMISM, HARD WORK, AND COMMONSENSE PROBLEM SOLVING.

I'm a problem solver, so I set out to determine the root cause of our issues at the patient-statement company and find a solution on my own. It didn't take long, and it wasn't hard. Most of our problems stemmed from simple human error—stuff that was very easy to correct. *Just a little more training*, I thought. Just a little more caring. Caring. Yeah, *that's* what was missing.

Very few of my coworkers seemed to care that we were losing customers or that our reputation was suffering. Was it because they didn't know how hings were? Or was it because they weren't the ones taking the heat from the customers? Was it because they were paid the same whether we lost an account or not? Maybe it was a combination of all those factors. Whatever the reason, the majority of the staff seemed oblivious to the problems. They just clocked in and clocked out without care or (immediate) consequence. In many ways, they were simply reflecting our CEO's own apathetic approach.

> **"No one cared about the company because no one cared about the employees."**

Then it hit me: *No one cared about the company because no one cared about the employees.* They weren't included in any discussions. They weren't asked what they needed to improve their performance. Heck, the leadership team members had their own separate entrance and separate restrooms. The only interaction we had with most of the employees was watching them from the picture window that looked down onto the production floor.

BUT OUR EMPLOYEES HAD THE SOLUTIONS

They had the knowledge. They had the answers. We just had to enlist their help. To get better, we had to find out what they knew, what they saw, and what they needed. We had to include them in the conversation and listen to them. We had to find a way to get them "engaged." I was fired up by this epiphany.

Excitedly, I went to my boss with suggestions for ways to improve morale and to get my coworkers in sync. My excitement was short-lived. My boss reacted by patting my hand and saying, "Sherry, you don't know anything about business. Just go sell another account."

How could it be that I cared so much, that I was such a dedicated, loyal employee doing everything in my power to make my boss's company successful, when he placed no value on my ideas and opinions? His reaction only reinforced my hypothesis: If he didn't care about *my* opinion (and I was the person responsible for our revenue), how much could he care about the employees who were operating the machines or stuffing envelopes? In that moment, I was crushed. But that moment would influence my future in big ways. It was a turning point.

Timing is everything. The day after that conversation, I was invited to have lunch with a highly successful entrepreneur who'd started and sold multiple businesses in the healthcare revenue cycle world. He said he'd been observing the company and me and was willing to bet on me. Big time. He offered me the opportunity to start a competing patient-statement company—one that he'd finance and in which I'd be able to earn up to 5 percent ownership over time.

To be sure, for me to be pursued by the entrepreneur in this way was a heady compliment. But he was offering me an annual starting salary of $35,000. At the time, I was making $16,000 a month. I wasn't willing to go backward, even for a bit of equity in the company. Further, my gut instinct told me that his investor style would not allow me to run the company the way I thought it should be run, and owning only 5 percent would not give me the power to make changes.

Though I turned down his offer, his interest filled me with confidence. I thought, *If HE believes in me, and he has been so successful, I should believe in myself more. Perhaps I should go out on my own.* What a catalyst his attention turned out to be!

Over the next few weeks, I mapped out what I needed to start a business. I didn't have much money but I did have a 401(k). Naïvely, I inquired about a bank loan and was turned down immediately. Financing didn't look promising, so I approached my boss again, hoping this time he'd listen to my ideas. He was just as dismissive as before. I was filled with righteous indignation and resigned. He made it easy to walk out the door and never walk back in again.

THE RETURNED MAIL
BUY-BACK GUARANTEE

At that point, I didn't consider any path other than starting my own business and controlling my own destiny. Just like that. It's funny now, but my boss was right when he said I didn't know anything about business. For example, I knew I needed a business plan, but the truth is, I'd never even *read* one, much less *written* one! So there I was, a few hours later, walking out of the bookstore with a stack of books about business plans tucked under my arm. I devoured them all.

Within a few days, I had crafted a very simple business plan—eleven or twelve pages long. Then I met with a now-defunct business that reviewed business plans, served as advisors, and sometimes invested when they saw potential. The two gentlemen were respectful and honest with their evaluation of my business idea:

> *"There's nothing here. There's nothing special. The industry is quickly maturing, with several huge companies already involved. It would be practically impossible for you to compete with them effectively. Your biggest asset is your knowledge of the industry and that you're well known within it, but that's not enough. You must either find a way to do something that no one else is doing—or solve a problem that no one has solved—or forget about starting this business."*

I was undeterred. I obsessed over what I could do to get a foothold in a mature market. Where or how could I bring value so potential customers would be willing to give us a try? In my head, I replayed every sales call I'd made in the previous years and every pain point I'd noticed along the way. What challenges were unaddressed?

One big problem kept popping up. Returned mail. That is, bins and bins of bills, hundreds of thousands of them, that hospitals had mailed to patients but that had been returned as "undeliverable" for various reasons: *No longer at this address; Moved, no forwarding address; No such street in this city;*

Forwarding order expired; No mail receptacle; etc. I recalled this problem happening repeatedly, both in rural hospitals and the big-city medical centers.

I started calling hospitals to ask a few questions: Was undeliverable mail a problem for them? If so, on what scale? What did they do with the returned mail? What was the overall cost of undelivered bills?

After a day of such calls, one large healthcare system invited me to visit to see for myself how big a problem undelivered mail was for them. They led me to a locked storage room that was filled with bins and boxes, six feet deep and six feet high. This one facility alone had tens of thousands of patient billing statements gathering dust and NOT collecting revenue.

As my research and phone interviews continued, I learned that hospitals experience as much as 15 percent returned mail because of bad patient addresses. They don't have the resources to track down correct addresses in a timely manner, so the debt is often turned over to a collection agency.

Turning the debt over to a third party can have negative consequences. The collection agencies have better tools and resources to locate good addresses, and once the addresses are obtained, they send a series of letters to the patient. This often means that the first written correspondence the patient receives from the hospital is a collection letter from a third party. Not only does it damage the hospital–patient relationship, it can also damage the patient's credit rating. When the payments are ultimately collected, the already cash-strapped hospital must then give a portion to the collection agency. In this scenario, the only winner is the collection agency.

I had identified the problem, but now I had to find the solution. I didn't sleep for three days. I stayed up studying every possible way around the issue. When the idea hit me, I immediately called two potential customers and pitched it to them. I tried the "If I . . . , Would You?" technique, and it worked. One answered, "This is the quintessential no-brainer. Of course, you can have our business if you can deliver on this promise!" The other prospect was less effusive in her praise for my idea but nevertheless agreed to give it a try.

BADA BING, BADA BOOM!

I had my first two clients: a large healthcare system in Memphis and a physician's group that was part of a large, prestigious healthcare system in Boston. I was on my way!

What was the solution to the problem that launched my business? A Returned Mail Buy-Back Guarantee. I promised to give the hospital a refund for every piece of mail that was returned to them, undelivered, for any reason.

Here's how it worked: We received the daily billing files from the hospital. Within just a few hours, we processed every patient address through multiple address cleansing and updating tools. We provided the customer (the hospital) with a report of all address changes. Then, that same day, we printed and mailed the patient bill to the right address the first time. If a good address was not available, we suppressed the bill from printing, notified the hospital, and received their permission to do further skip-tracing searches for the individual. Working on the honor system, the client provided a count of the pieces that were returned, and we issued a full refund, postage and all.

With two new hospital contracts in hand, I rushed back to the local banks to seek the seed money to fund the business. Once again, I was turned down. Apparently, I wasn't "bankable."

I'd just have to fund it myself!

First, I cashed in my 401(k). Next, much to the dismay of my classy neighbors, I put my house on the market and held a week-long yard sale. I sold most of my personal belongings and kept only the essentials. Watching every penny, I went to Goodwill to buy the basic things I needed to establish an office. I was able to find two short filing cabinets for $17. Then I found a cheap old door that I placed across the top of the filing cabinets and—voilà—I had a desk! With a secondhand whiteboard, an old computer, and a landline, I began working sixteen hours a day.

For the first several weeks, I referred to my business as Mail Magnates, but

I had to spell both words for people and explain that, no, I was not claiming to be a *man magnet*! I soon came up with a better name. LetterLogic was born and took off like a rocket! Within a few short weeks, I went from being a disgruntled employee to being a CEO. I was going to build my company, my way. I had discovered the missing ingredient in business—caring. Caring was going to be the cornerstone of my business model and leadership style for every interaction moving forward: with clients, with vendors, and with everyone who came on board to help me build the company.

TAKEAWAY BOX:

Don't keep beating on a door that has closed. Sometimes that door is right beside a wall that has fallen down. Climb on out!

Second Course

SHARED PLATES

4

Lunch with Lucy
Getting to the Heart of the Matter

"You learn a lot about someone when you share a meal together."

–Anthony Bourdain

INGREDIENTS:

SHUT UP AND LISTEN.

A n odd thing happens when you have the title of CEO. People think you're "somebody" and they treat you differently. Though I'm aware of the power the title carries, I felt the enormous responsibility that accompanies it when I took a new employee out to lunch one day. We had driven less than a mile when I noticed she was nervous, shaking even.

I asked, "Alicia, are you okay? Is something the matter?"

"Yes," she replied. "I've never been out to lunch with a CEO before. I'm very nervous I will say or do something wrong."

Wow. I pulled the car over to the side of the road, shifted to park, and then turned in my seat so I could look her square in the eye.

"Alicia, you need to understand that I'm just a regular person. The only reason I have the title CEO is because I started a company and I could choose any title I wanted. That seemed to be a good one."

I went on to explain my background to her, that I had scrubbed toilets for a living, and that I only had a high school education. I told her that due to her education and experience in IT, I was in awe of *her*. Her nervousness didn't go away immediately, but she relaxed a little and we were able to have a fun lunch together.

> "...to be a true 'people first' organization... I had to know my employees better."

I realized that to be a true "people first" organization, based on an empathetic leadership business model as I had resolved to be from day one, I had to know my employees better. We needed to get beyond the superficial water-cooler conversations and get to know each other's struggles and dreams and aspirations. How could I claim we were a family if we knew nothing about each other's lives? What were their situations at home? What were the specific circumstances they dealt with every day before coming to work to help build our company?

The LetterLogic team had grown to over thirty full-time employees. We were growing rapidly, spread across a 27,000-square-foot factory. But we were beginning to lose the intimacy and closeness of the early years. So I set out to create a regular, informal occasion where I could get one-on-one time with each employee to *truly* get to know them. Lunch seemed like a good idea.

THE LUCY BASICS:
MAKING EVERY EMPLOYEE FEEL VALUED

I came up with the moniker "Lucy" as a substitute for Sherry. I wanted to remove any anxiety the employees might feel about having lunch with

Sherry Deutschmann, the CEO of LetterLogic. I wanted to encourage them to think of me as a coworker, not the boss.

At our next company meeting, I introduced myself as Lucy and explained the lunch concept to my coworkers. They loved it and immediately clamored to get on Lucy's calendar. So, for a few hours each Wednesday, I took off my CEO hat, and any employee who wanted to could choose to "Lunch with Lucy." Though I chose the name "Lucy" because I like alliteration and the way it flowed with Lunch, and LetterLogic, it stuck, and now, years later, I get emails and texts addressed to "Lucy."

I chose Wednesdays because it was typically our low-volume day. Even if my lunch companion was on the production team—where timing is critical—they could likely get away for an hour without affecting the rest of the team. On most other weekdays, I had lunch appointments with clients, potential clients, or mentors and mentees. Our employees knew this, because I often brought anyone I was having lunch with through the facility for a quick tour. By reserving my Wednesday lunch hour for our employees, I let them know they were just as important as our bankers, lawyers, and clients.

The Lunch with Lucy guidelines were simple. First, the employee chose the restaurant. If I'd been the one to choose where we ate, I probably would have

"The only person who mattered was the person I was sharing lunch with..."

picked one of my regular lunch places, which meant that I knew several of the other regular patrons and waitstaff. Inevitably, one or two people would stop by to say hello, and even with the best intentions, suddenly the lunch would be all about me—which was the exact opposite of what I wanted to happen. So, rule number one was that the employee picked the place.

The second rule was that I chose the least prominent chair at the table. If we were seated at a booth or small table, I took the seat with my back to the door or to the other patrons. Most type-A entrepreneurs are accustomed to choosing the seat that allows them to see who else is in the room or who else enters the room. But on Wednesdays, and to Lucy, those other people didn't matter. The only person who mattered was the person I was sharing lunch with, so I positioned myself to be free of distractions.

We've all attended those luncheons where the host holds court and acts as if the world revolves around them. As Lucy, I wanted to avoid that trap and deliberately created circumstances that let my guests know my attention would be on them. Once the seating was sorted out, my goal was to get my lunch companion to open up and tell me about their lives. I believe there are a few key factors that invite people to feel comfortable with me.

Why Employees Let Their Guard Down with Me

1. I genuinely care about people. I have innate empathy for others, and sometimes it drives me crazy. If I go to a football game and my team wins, of course I am elated and want to celebrate with the throngs of people around me. But inevitably, I glance over at the losing team and am crushed for them. Suddenly, I can't celebrate anymore. In a matter of seconds, I'm wiping away tears for the people who lost. I'm the first to admit that this is empathy to the extreme, but I care for others, and I believe people sense that.

2. I ask a lot of questions.

3. Then I shut up and listen.

4. Listening is key to being a good leader. No doubt, there might be a few people who knew me years ago who are gagging in disbelief. Listening is something I learned to do—not something I did instinctively. I had to work on it and practice.

5. When appropriate, I share little bits of self-revelatory information to demonstrate I'm letting down my guard and they
are safe doing the same. I don't share more for no other reason
than, in this setting, it is all about them.

6. If all else fails, I go back to number 3. I shut up and listen.

The third rule was that the employee got to decide if our lunch would
be just the two of us, or if they wanted to include others—another team
member, a friend from outside the company, their entire department—it
was all up to them.

THE LUCY CONVERSATIONS:
LAYING THE GROUNDWORK

One of the most memorable "Lunch with Lucy" sessions was not a lunch
at all. It started with a young employee I'll call Charles who asked me to
have lunch with him and his mother. His mom was moving to Hawaii and
was concerned about leaving her son behind, so far away from her. I gladly
agreed to the lunch, anxious to meet Charles's mom and let her know I'd
watch out for him.

Just a few days before our lunch date, Charles asked if we could invite a few
others and make it a dinner instead. I agreed. The dinner turned into a fun,
lively, beer-enhanced evening that included his mom, his brother, a room-
mate, and a few of his coworkers, which added up to ten of us in all. We ended
the night with hugs all around, and a mom who felt more confident moving
because she'd met her son's "boss" and declared me a surrogate mom.

Having met his mother and friends, I got a better sense of who Charles
was and how to best support him in his role at LetterLogic. This type of

knowledge can only come in a relaxed environment where people feel empowered to be themselves.

Not everyone opens up as easily as Charles did. With some of my employees, I had to work a little harder to get them to trust me and feel comfortable sharing where they were coming from. Lincoln Atwood was one of those people.

A senior developer/architect, Lincoln is one of the most gifted IT professionals you'll ever meet. With his long blond hair, beard, and Harley-Davidson gear, he looks more like an outlaw musician than a tech wizard. When I hired him, he was a single father to his pre-teen daughter, Austin. There are a million-and-one reasons I love Lincoln, but the single-parent thing always moves me. Been there. Done that. It's difficult.

Getting to know Lincoln was also a little difficult. He was an independent contractor we had brought in for an eighteen-month stint. He preferred contract work and had no plans to stay with us beyond his contract. He seemed leery of me for quite a while, and it took months before he would talk openly with me. But over time, we started sharing lunch (or breakfast) regularly as a result of my Lunch with Lucy tradition. As Lucy, I got to see that, despite his tough biker persona, Lincoln was a complete softy—especially when it came to his daughter. Then he started dating Valerie. I don't know how many meals I spent with Lincoln talking about Valerie until she finally agreed to marry him!

Here's the thing: If it hadn't been for the Lunch with Lucy custom, Lincoln would just be that smart guy who worked downstairs for eighteen months and left at the end of his contract. He would never have engaged with us fully, and I wouldn't have gotten to know him as a kindhearted family man. But he didn't leave us. He came to appreciate his work family and chose to stick with us. Eight years later, he was still with me at LetterLogic and happy to be there.

Aside from the opportunity for me to get to know my employees, Lunch with Lucy was good for me for other reasons. Because of Lunch with Lucy,

I probably had lunch with Harvey McClendon more than anyone else. Harvey was the custodian, gatekeeper, confidant to all, and in-house therapist at LetterLogic. He frequently popped into my office for an impromptu Lunch with Lucy. "Hey, you wanna try the best gyros in town?" or "That place up the street has some great fried chicken—want to give it a shot?"

We often ate lunch in my office, with our meals on little tables pulled up to the sofa. Harvey became my mentor and parenting coach. He never pulled any punches with me, advising and admonishing me when he felt I was being too critical or impatient. I needed and valued his advice and support. To this day, Harvey and I meet for lunch regularly. We built a lifelong friendship that I value dearly. Lucy started it all.

THE LUCY EFFECT: INSIGHTS INTO YOUR COMPANY

Sometimes Lunch with Lucy was an opportunity for employees to get me away from the office and talk about something they wanted or needed. The importance of a program that invited transparency was invaluable, as I found out so many times. We'd spend a few hours hashing out whatever they were worried about and come up with a plan to fix it. Most of the time, the issues they raised were important. The lunch forum gave me the chance to meet with and listen to them. Without it, I might have lost some valuable team members.

For example, for a few years, we had a policy that guaranteed a forty-hour workweek for all non-salaried employees. A new manager decided it was too generous[2] and changed the policy. The impact on morale was

---

2   Our workload was heavily skewed to the beginning of the week, with Monday the high-volume day, sometimes requiring ten and twelve hours. But midweek, the volume was much lower and the workers had short days and could go home several hours earlier. By guaranteeing pay for forty hours even if they actually only worked thirty-six, they didn't mind those extra-long Mondays. And they didn't try to "milk the clock" on the other days—they just completed the daily load, set up for the following day, and went off to enjoy the afternoon on their own. Without us prodding and pleading, they adjusted their personal circumstances to stay as long as they were needed, knowing that we'd make it up to them on the other days.

immediate and palpable. One of the production teams asked Lucy to lunch to talk about the policy change. Over a two-hour meal, the team members laid out their case for why the policy change was damaging to them and to the company. I listened. I agreed with them, and we reinstated the original rules.

I recall at least two occasions when employees chose Lunch with Lucy to tell me they were leaving LetterLogic for a new career. You might think I'm crazy, but those were happy, proud moments. It's like seeing your kid go off to college. You'll miss them being around, but you know they're growing and learning and expanding their horizons. It was my job and privilege to see my employees leave the nest and move on to bigger and better things. Lunch with Lucy made it possible for them to talk honestly and openly about the next stage in their professional growth and to get my blessing. It was our practice to throw a going-away party for anyone who left, the reason being that we believed it gave them confidence for their next adventure.

THE LUCY INVESTMENT: YOUR COMPANY'S GREATEST ASSET

Lunch with Lucy was more than bonding time. Those lunches were beneficial to the company culture to be sure, but they also added to our bottom line. They helped us retain great employees who could have easily gone elsewhere.

For several years, Nashville has experienced extraordinary growth, especially in the technology sector, with new companies opening shop daily. IT professionals, even those fresh out of school, are in great demand, commanding surprisingly high starting salaries. At the time of this writing, there were over one thousand IT jobs available in Nashville. As soon as you hire a great candidate, they immediately start receiving phone calls, emails, and LinkedIn messages from recruiters offering them more money or ridiculous perks to leave you. It's maddening!

Studies on employee turnover estimate the cost to be as high as 15 percent to 25 percent of the position's annual salary. There's the time it takes to find a replacement, the lost opportunity cost during the lag time, and the cost to recruit and train a new employee. Losing an IT staff member making $80,000+ annually is very impactful because of the length of time it takes for a new hire to navigate the custom technology platform well enough to be contributing fully.

My strategy for minimizing turnover was to create a work environment where people wanted to stay, even if they were offered more money somewhere else. There is no doubt in my mind that Lunch with Lucy contributed to creating such an environment. Because our employees connected with us on a very personal level, they were less susceptible to being poached because they loved being part of Lucy's family.

Here are just some of the ways that getting to really know your employees will serve you, your organization, and your staff.

When You Really Get to Know Your Employees

- You'll get to know the extraordinary people you've entrusted to do the work of your company.

- You'll be able to express your gratitude face-to-face.

- You'll learn what motivates them and how they like to be rewarded.

- You'll learn where to remove barriers that prevent them from being as effective as they can be in their jobs.

- You'll become a more attentive, attuned coworker because you'll learn about what keeps people up at night and what they most dread or most look forward to.

continued

- You'll see your employees in a new light. That insight will help you be a better leader.

- You'll build relationships that garner loyalty. With loyalty, you'll retain your employees even when other companies try to lure them away.

- When you retain your employees because they are happy and feel connected to you, they produce better work. Better work leads to happy customers. Happy customers are loyal, and willing to pay more for your services and products. They are willing to weather a few difficult storms and stick with you when things don't go as planned.

- You'll get a better understanding of your company's inner workings. You'll learn what equipment needs to be replaced. Or not. You'll learn about that one little inefficiency that creates half a dozen opportunities for errors down the line.

- You'll learn when your leaders are truly leading and developing their teams. Or not.

- Once you really engage with your team members, you'll find that each one of them becomes part of the sales team. They are the ones who make or break the company's reputation in the community. They affect your brand more than any other factor.

- You'll be able to run a tighter, more aligned organization, which absolutely creates a healthier bottom line, which means you'll be more profitable.

I'll be the first to admit that Lunch with Lucy probably mattered more to Lucy than to anyone else. I treasured this time with the people who were working hard to make us a great company. Would a tradition like Lunch with Lucy matter to your company? Here's the thing: You can spend tens of thousands of dollars on a consultant to gauge the effectiveness of your leadership and evaluate your company culture. Or, you can spend $40 on lunch and get the word directly from the horse's mouth. The choice is yours.

TAKEAWAY BOX:

Create and guard every opportunity to LISTEN to your employees. Get to know their dreams, their goals, their struggles, and what they need to be better at their jobs—and to have a better life.

5

Meat & Potatoes
Fair Living Wages

"I don't pay good wages because I have a lot of money. I have a lot of money because I pay good wages."

–Robert Bosch

INGREDIENTS:

FAIR PAY IS EVERY ENTREPRENEUR'S
PRIVILEGE . . . AND RESPONSIBILITY.

In Tennessee as of October 2018, the minimum wage was $7.25 an hour. A full-time employee paid minimum wage grossed $290 a week. Appropriate use of the word "gross" don't you think? Don't get me started! Even in 2002, when LetterLogic launched, $7.25 an hour was just not acceptable. For the first several years, our starting hourly wage in the factory was $12 an hour, and we thought we were being generous. But one day, I heard something that struck a chord so loudly I had to make some changes.

During a leadership conference, an executive from a public company shared how they defined a "fair living wage." They considered this hypothetical situation: "What if the two lowest-paid employees started dating and ultimately got married? On their joint salaries, in what part of town could they afford to live? Could they buy a home or must they always rent? Would they be able to save any money? Could they afford to start a family? Could they afford to put money aside for their children's education? Could they take real vacations?" Using those criteria, his company established a standard "fair living wage" in each market.

Wow. I was stunned. And worried.

I hurried back to the office and met with our CFO. We reviewed our compensation policy against the inspiring fair living wage standard I had just learned about. It was obvious we weren't paying enough to meet the standard. My knee-jerk reaction was to raise the minimum wage to $14 immediately. After a few more weeks of studying the situation and several sleepless nights, we made another adjustment and raised our starting minimum wage to $16 an hour.

> " . . . Paying a fair living wage was the foundation for employee engagement, and that paved the way to our success."

When all was said and done, several people received raises of $2 or more. A few received $4 more per hour. Of course they were happy! Interestingly though, the person who showed the most appreciation for the raise was Nancy. Before the increase, her pay rate was $15.99. Even though she only received a $0.01 raise, she was grateful. Her gratitude was due to her own keenly developed sense of empathy. She celebrated that her coworkers were taking home more money.

Our commitment to paying a fair living wage brought LetterLogic a lot of attention. I even received a call and a visit from Tom Perez, then US Secretary of Labor. He wanted to talk about the effect our policies were having on profitability. Secretary Perez had worked tirelessly to increase the federal minimum wage, and his opponents were certain that doing so would devastate small businesses' bottom line, force layoffs, and drive unemployment up.

I was happy to tell Secretary Perez that our experience proved his opponents wrong. In the eighteen months following our starting pay raise from $12 to $16 an hour, our profitability quadrupled! That is not a misprint. We quadrupled our earnings before interest, taxes, depreciation and amortization (EBIDTA).

Of course, the wage increase was not the only change we made. We made other smart investments too, but paying a fair living wage was the foundation for employee engagement, and that paved the way to our success.

MINIMUM WAGE VERSUS FAIR LIVING WAGE: AN ILLUSTRATION

Who do you envision when you think about minimum-wage workers? High school kids bagging groceries? College students flipping burgers? Yes, minimum wage workers do tend to be young, with workers from ages sixteen to twenty-four making up 50 percent of this income bracket. But surprisingly, single moms are overrepresented in this low-income category too. According to the 2017 US Census Bureau, 80 percent of one-parent families in our country are led by women, and sadly, 40 percent of *their* children live in poverty.

After her wages were raised to $16 an hour, one of my employees told me it was the first time in her fifty-two years that she made enough money to work just one job. The first time in her life! Yet she used her newfound freedom and time to take care of her grandchildren so their mother could work a second job. This cycle has to change.

The reality of living on minimum wage is entirely unsustainable. To illustrate this truth, let's follow a day in the life of a thirty-five-year-old single mom with a six-year-old son and a twelve-year-old daughter.

Mom leaves the house at 7:30 a.m., runs to catch the bus, and arrives at her $7.25-an-hour job just in time to punch in at 8:00 a.m. She's already tired because she didn't sleep well and knows it's going to be a long day. Her workday ends at 4:00 p.m. She made a whopping $58.

She takes the bus home and walks into the sweltering, tiny apartment she rents in a dangerous neighborhood. She's there just long enough to kiss her kids, change into her uniform, and head out to her second job. Sadly, Mom can't stay to cook dinner, or help them with homework, or to see that they bathe and brush their teeth, or read them bedtime stories. Why? Because by 5:30 p.m., she has clocked in at her second job.

On the clock at her second job, she is so tired that she falls asleep twice in front of her supervisor! She knows she needs to do better if she wants to keep this job, and she *has* to keep this job. At 1:00 a.m., she finally clocks out. She made another $50.

Back home, Mom turns the key in the lock to see that, once again, the kids have fallen asleep in front of the TV. She doesn't have the heart or energy to wake them, so she tiptoes past them and falls, exhausted, onto her bed. It's 1:30 a.m., and she has only six hours before the whole cycle starts over again.

How does Mom look to her two employers? Her daytime employer is fed up with her, because he knows she's bright, and he knows she's not lazy, but she just can't seem to focus. She makes the same mistakes over and over again. He's going to give her one last chance to shape up.

The nighttime employer is at her breaking point. She covers for Mom because she knows she has a hard life, but she can't tolerate her falling asleep at her workstation. The quality of her work is getting worse. Mom repeatedly asks for a raise, but how can you give someone a raise when they sleep on the job?

How are the kids affected by Mom working two jobs? They've learned to fend for themselves. Their meals consist of breakfast bars and microwave dinners. They're both getting poor grades and having a hard time concentrating in class. After school, they spend hours watching TV and playing video games. They can't play outside because the neighborhood is not safe.

Do you get the picture?

Let's do the math. Mom is working two jobs at minimum wage. Her gross pay is $543 a week—$28,236 a year before taxes—which is why she lives in an $800 a month dump with no air conditioning. She can't afford childcare. She struggles to make ends meet. She can never get ahead.

How can an employee be expected to come to work with a great attitude *and* focus and produce high-quality goods and services when all they can think about is if the electricity will be cut off at home? How can Mom be a good employee or a decent parent or a contributing member of the community if she is constantly exhausted?

Recently, a handful of states (and even almighty Amazon) raised the minimum wage to $15 an hour. In 2019, a total of twenty-two states initiated minimum wage increases: Washington DC raised their rate to $14, Massachusetts to $12, and Washington state to $12. These and several other states have built-in increases over the next few years that will bring them all to from $13 to $15 per hour. On the other end of the scale, Georgia and Wyoming stand together with minimum wage at a paltry $5.15 per hour.[3]

Now, let's consider how Mom's life might improve with a higher wage. She wakes up and makes the kids some hot oatmeal and blueberries before she walks them to the bus stop. Then she hurries over to her job, clocking in ten minutes before 8:00 a.m. to get a cup of coffee with her coworkers. She's well rested and focused. Her employer thinks she's a great worker. At lunch, she's able to take a walk through the neighborhood for a little sunshine and exercise before she begins her afternoon of work. She clocks out at 4:30 p.m., happy to get home to see the kids. Today she earned $120.

---

3   National Conference of State Legislatures. "State Minimum Wages, 2019 Minimum Wages by State." http://www.ncsl.org/research/labor-and-employment/state-minimum-wage-chart.aspx

Back at home, she sits down at the kitchen table to help the kids with their homework. Then she prepares a healthy dinner for them. At bedtime, she's tucking two happy, well-fed, scrubbed kids into bed before she's able to relax and take a bath herself. It's still early, not yet 9:00, so she has time to focus on the online class she's taking. Once she gets her degree, she'll be eligible for a higher-paying job.

I KNOW WHAT IT'S LIKE

Can you feel the difference? You can smell it and taste it! Mom's not going to get rich on $15 an hour, but she can finally have a life. Though my imagination can take me to that sweltering apartment, I don't really need to imagine her hardship. I lived it. I know what it's like to want to be a good employee but not be able to concentrate. I know how stressful it was when the car was so low on gas that I worried about making it to daycare to pick up my daughter. That's the daycare I hadn't even paid for yet. And when I did find enough change to put a gallon of gas in the car and pick up my daughter, we came home to a hot, dark apartment because the power bill wasn't paid and our electricity was turned off.

" ... if you find good employees and pay them a fair living wage, you'll be rewarded with better products and services."

I can't promise that paying your employees more will cause your profits to quadruple, or even double. But I can guarantee that if you find good employees and pay them a fair living wage, you'll be rewarded with better products and services. When your products and services are superior, people will pay more for them. When people pay more, you'll take more to the bottom line. It's as simple as that.

HOW FAIR PAY CHANGES LIVES

Time and time again, we saw how fair pay affected the lives of our employees and their communities. The story of Maria is the best example. She and her husband immigrated to the United States from Mexico, and both worked full-time jobs. Maria's job required her to work twelve hours a day, six days a week. She's lucky she had a relative to help with childcare until her husband could get home from work.

When Maria came to LetterLogic, her family life and future were forever altered. She was paid a fair living wage for a reasonable forty-hour workweek. Since her husband no longer had to rush home to take care of the children to accommodate her extra-long workdays, he could take on more overtime at his high-paying, skilled construction job. For the first time, they were able to save money.

By living on the husband's income and saving Maria's pay, the couple paid off their vehicles. They bought a house! They had another child. They are model citizens investing in the community. Paying Maria a fair living wage was a vital part of the ecosystem that made such life dreams possible. And Maria, a dedicated, hardworking, consistent, reliable employee, was worth every penny.

What about the argument that companies won't be as profitable, layoffs will spike, and unemployment will rise if minimum wage is increased? You can find studies that show that raising the minimum wage has no negative effect

> "Look at your employees and imagine your life if you were paid what they are being paid."

on the nation's economy when done in moderate increments—and studies that argue the opposite. So, I'll resort to my own commonsense approach here. Forget about what anyone else is paying. Look at your employees and imagine your life if you were paid what they are being paid. How dramatically would your lifestyle change? How dedicated would you be to an employer who pays what you are paying?

Consider our single mom. When paid a fair living wage, she is able to make ends meet with just one job. She is able to take better care of herself and her children. She is also able to perform better at work, and her employer takes notice. Coincidentally, she's able to quit that second nighttime job, *leaving it open for someone else.* She now has money to spend, which puts dollars back into the local economy, which creates jobs!

WHEN OTHERS PAY LOW WAGES, IT AFFECTS ALL OF US

Consider now what happens at companies that pay consistently low wages. Recently, I went to a big-box store with my daughter. It's owned by the wealthiest family in the world—you know the one.

On the positive side, the store was clean and well organized. But the customer service couldn't have been much worse. There were dozens of employees milling about aimlessly, and not one of them was willing to assist me. On one aisle, two employees were throwing a package of toilet paper back and forth to each other. They seemed aggravated when they had to suspend their game for a few seconds to allow me to pass through.

Over in the fabric department, I couldn't find anyone to cut the length of material I had selected. After waiting fifteen minutes for someone to appear, I went in search of help. I found two managers leaning on a display case chatting, and just beyond them, seven (seven!) employees were lounging around talking to each other. I patiently waited for the managers to acknowledge us, standing three feet away, but they didn't, so I politely interrupted and asked for help. Without looking at me, the manager called for someone on the intercom to go to the fabric department. I went back to that area and waited.

One by one, a total of five different individuals showed up, but not one offered to help me and not one had the ability to open the register. None of them had been trained how to cut fabric either, so we still had to wait.

Several minutes later, an employee came over to cut the fabric, but not until after she had complained about having to do so.

Things did not improve at checkout. The cashier never once looked at me or spoke a word to me. Not even the usual "paper or plastic?" Instead, she and a coworker were busy complaining about their work schedules. I paid for the items, bagged them myself, and left, hopefully never to return.

It's common knowledge that this particular big-box store pays low wages, so low that the American taxpayers (you and I) subsidize their employees' pay through food stamps and other programs to the tune of over $6 billion a year.[4] Did you get that? The employees are paid so poorly that you and I pay higher taxes just to help them survive. It's a fact.

The ironic truth is that the employers (those rich folks) are affected as well. So few of their employees are truly engaged that it takes two to three times as many employees to get the basic tasks completed. So instead of paying one employee $15 an hour, they have to pay two or three employees $8.25 an hour. How does that make any sense? Even those big-box stores would benefit financially if they just took better care of their people.

TAKEAWAY BOX:

When your employees make enough money to cover their basic needs, they are better able to focus, take care of your customers, and be engaged in their work.

---

4   Clare O'Connor. "Report: Walmart Workers Costs Taxpayers $6.2 Billion in Public Assistance," *Forbes*, April 15, 2014, https://www.forbes.com/sites/clareoconnor/2014/04/15/report-walmart-workers-cost-taxpayers-6-2-billion-in-public-assistance/#6177f887720b

6

A Piece of the Pie
A Profit Sharing Plan
That Drives Profitability

"Our most valuable possessions are those which can be shared without lessening–those which, when shared, multiply."

–William H. Danforth

> INGREDIENTS:
>
> A PROFIT SHARING PLAN THAT
> GENERATES EVEN GREATER PROFITS.

P rofit sharing plans are not new. Many companies offer them, and they are a good way to reward employees when the company does well. In my opinion, though, most plans are too complex and too convoluted for the average employee to understand.

Typical profit sharing plans tend to have the same basic characteristics:

- They are based on annual profit, so the payout is also annual and usually distributed in the second quarter.

- The money is pooled and distributed using various formulas, usually as a percentage of a person's base salary. That is: The higher your salary, the more of the pool you get.

The typical profit sharing model didn't appeal to me. I didn't want to just reward good results. My goal was to *guarantee* good results with a plan that would drive engagement and affect behavior. Instead of looking at the profit share as a payout or dividend, I considered it an investment.

By *investing* in our employees, we were able to maximize profitability in a way that no other approach could achieve, which created a much larger pie with ever-growing profits. The plan was simple enough that it made sense to anyone we hired, and it truly did influence behavior, unlike any other profit share plan I've ever seen.

> "Instead of looking at the profit share as a payout or dividend, I considered it an investment."

STEP ONE: MONTHLY DISTRIBUTION

To ensure good results and drive engagement, Step one was to measure *monthly* profits and make the *distributions monthly* too. I made this commitment knowing—especially in the early days—that we could have a non-profitable month right after a profitable one. I was willing to take the risk for three reasons:

- I was trying to affect behavior. I wanted the employees to see the direct correlation between their actions/behaviors/decisions and the results. When profit distribution was done every thirty days, it was easy for them to remember the events—good or bad—that led to a profit or a loss. The timeliness allowed them to associate cause and effect and take corrective action immediately.

- Annual rewards are too far off, too nebulous, to be real to most employees. Monthly payouts—distributed no later than the sixteenth day of each month—now, that was concrete. And motivating!

- How many times have you heard someone confess they're only staying with a company until the bonuses are paid or the profit share is distributed, and then they're out the door? How many employees are just putting in their time to get to the big payoff day while they are actively disengaged or not contributing? By distributing the profit share monthly, we were able to weed out bad hires sooner and recoup losses faster.

STEP TWO: THIS WILL SHOCK YOU

Step two is radical, so have a seat.

Not only did we make the profit distributions monthly; we made them identical across the board. The receptionist and the CFO and the equipment operators got the exact same dollar amount as the COO and the junior programmer and the custodian. This showed every single person that their job and their role was just as important as any other.

> "Not only did we make the profit distributions monthly; we made them identical across the board."

An even distribution of the profit share was absolutely critical to morale and engagement for several reasons:

- A bad receptionist can do irreparable harm to the company brand with just one exasperated or curt phone conversation.

- No matter how brilliant our technology, one careless move on the production floor could wipe out a month's profit.

- No matter how sharp our programmers and code writers were, they were only human. They could make mistakes that had a significant impact on the customer and the company.

- The actions (or inactions) of the rank and file members of our organization could make or break us as easily as a slipup by a member of the executive team.

- It demonstrated clearly that every one of us played an equally valuable role.

The Dreaded Double-Stuff
(This is not about Oreos.)

Let me give you a real-life example of how sharing the profits changed behavior.

One of the essential pieces of machinery in our industry is an inserter. At its most basic functionality, an inserter folds and stuffs the paper statement into the outgoing envelope. Depending on how it's programmed, an inserter can also include a remittance envelope and any number of marketing materials in the outgoing envelope as well. It's fun to watch the machine grab a sheet of paper, fold it in exactly the right spot, slide it along to the envelope, which is then opened, filled, closed, and sealed at the rate of 8,000 to 12,000 per hour. This machine and this step in the process holds one of the greatest potential liabilities in our industry. If not operated properly, the inserter can create an outcome we call a "double-stuff."

A double-stuff is when two or more statements addressed to different individuals are inadvertently inserted into one envelope. In the healthcare industry, a double-stuff is a potential violation of federally mandated HIPAA (Health Insurance Portability and Accountability Act) regulations. In practical terms, a double-stuff means that a stranger receives their medical bill with *your* medical bill tucked in with it. Your bill might include your diagnosis, treatment, medications, and even payment history. Not only has your privacy been violated, but also, the company responsible for the mistake is subject to hefty fines on top of irreparable damage to its reputation.

Ironically, inserting machines have multiple mechanisms to prevent double-stuffs. In theory, a double-stuff just shouldn't happen. The reality is, the operator can override every mechanism and every fail-safe at their discretion.

Why in the world would an operator override the mechanisms that were designed to ensure every piece reconciled perfectly? There could be many reasons:

- They're human.

- They have a date tonight and need to leave early to get ready.

- They have a headache and are ready for the workday to be over.

- They're frustrated that the machine keeps giving false error codes.

- They believe the manual count is good enough *just this once.*

- They didn't fully understand the consequences of their actions.

- They didn't care, maybe, just maybe, *because they didn't have a vested interest in the outcome.*

Would profit sharing make a difference in how much an operator cared? I believed it would. LetterLogic's processes

continued

were identical to those used by our competitors. We all used the same or similar software. We owned the same or similar equipment. The key differentiator was that *every inserter operator* at LetterLogic received an equal share of the profits. They clearly understood how a double-stuff affected profitability. And they knew their failure to correct a mistake would affect not only their own income but their coworkers' incomes as well. Evenly distributed monthly profit share was a simple, clean way to get every individual vested in the outcome of his or her own actions.

I can't claim we never had a double-stuff, but it was a rare occasion. When we did have one, we *all* felt the pain. We saw how vital the inserter operators were to our final product and to our overall profitability. It was clear their profit share should absolutely be on par with that of any other employee. Doesn't that make sense?

STEP THREE:
THE FINAL FEATURE: MAKE IT TANGIBLE

A final feature of our profit sharing model was that we distributed *paper checks* to each employee at our monthly company meeting. Of course, we could have added profit share to the regular payroll with the automatic bank deposit, but I wanted everyone to have a *tangible* reward, right in the palm of their hands, to show them what they accomplished individually and what we accomplished together. There was no need for secrecy because we all got the same amount. Nonetheless, we all tore into those envelopes. Whether the checks were for $17 or $717, the celebration was loud and raucous.

Are you silently balking at the idea of giving away 10 percent of your profit, even though you might be a very generous person? Stop for a minute. What are you afraid of? Would you rather have the money for yourself? What's the point of that? You'll just pay more in taxes. Or, are you one of those entrepreneurs who believes you must reinvest every dime of profit back into your company? Do you think your company won't grow as quickly if you push 10 percent to the people who are responsible for that growth to begin with?

Listen. Your company will grow *faster* because you're investing in your greatest asset—your people. When you invest in your people by giving them 10 percent of the pie, you'll watch that pie get bigger (and better) month after month. There is no better return on investment (ROI).

THE PROOF IS IN THE PUDDING (OR, IN THIS CASE, THE PAPER)

The mechanics of LetterLogic's profit sharing policy were simple. We took 10 percent of the monthly bottom line and divided it equally by the number of eligible employees. (Employees were eligible after six months of employment.)

For example, if we had $200,000 net profit in a month, we paid out $20,000 in profit share the following month. Each of our fifty-three employees received a profit share of $377.36. For someone who made $18 an hour, the profit share added $2 per hour to their income. Who wouldn't be incentivized by that?

Over time, as our top line continued to grow and push the bottom line higher, the profit share checks got larger and larger. The last profit share checks I signed were over $1,000 per employee (a month)!

I've shared our profit sharing model with thousands of business owners over the past few years, and I'm surprised how often entrepreneurs question my decision to include our salespeople in the profit share pool. In fact, I've been admonished that salespeople should not be eligible to participate because they are already the highest paid individuals in the company. I strongly disagree.

In most businesses, commission is the bulk of the sales team's compensation. But too often, a salesperson will close a sale and be paid a commission for new business that will not benefit the company because the pricing was wrong or the scope of work was outside the company's core strengths. What better way to incentivize salespeople to acquire the perfect customer at the highest price than by giving them a share of the profit in addition to commission? Why should they be excluded? They take all the risk and spend days and days on the road away from their families.

> "Listen. Your company will grow *faster* because you're investing in your greatest asset—your people."

TAKEAWAY BOX:

Nothing will affect behavior and inspire engagement more effectively than a carefully designed profit sharing plan with timely payouts. When your employees have a vested interest in the success of the company, everybody wins.

7

Amish Friendship Bread
Pass It Around

"Bread for myself is a material question. Bread for my neighbor is a spiritual one."

–Nikolai Berdyaev

INGREDIENTS:

EMPATHY IS CONTAGIOUS.

The culture that thrived at LetterLogic was about more than fair wages, profit sharing, and empathetic communication. Our culture was the air we breathed. It was a palpable, contagious feeling we got each morning when we walked in the door and greeted our work family. We truly cared for each other. The positive environment we nurtured made our employees' personal lives better. At the end of the business day, we sent home better fathers, better mothers, better sisters, better brothers, better sons, better daughters, and better community members.

I've heard it said that a mother is only as happy as her least happy child. As one of seven children, that saying really resonated with me. Over the last sixty years, there have only been a few times when my mom could breathe a sigh of relief knowing all her children were doing well in all facets of their lives.

My mom, Doris Grey Beamon Stewart, is a quiet, reserved woman. I used to think she was quiet because it was so hard to get a word in edgewise among her children. But I've come to understand that she is quiet by nature. She is observant: responsive instead of reactive. Through the years, she has displayed an uncanny knack for knowing, without us having to tell her, when we needed her. And when she came to our rescue, there was no fanfare. No guilt. No lectures. She just quietly and humbly helped us.

> "I also wanted to inspire my work family to look out for one another and be quietly alert to challenges or problems that others may face."

Though I credit my father for my entrepreneurial spirit, I credit my mom for my emotional intelligence (EQ) and sixth sense. She was my model for how I attended to the needs of the LetterLogic family. I wanted to show the same kind of care that my mom showed us. I also wanted to inspire my work family to look out for one another and be quietly alert to challenges or problems that others may face. And they did. Time and time again.

THE FIRST-CLASS COMPANY WITH A HEART

The kindness and well, love, that we felt and showed our coworkers became part of the fabric of who we were. So much so that it became part of our brand. We became known as "LetterLogic—*the first class company with a heart.*" And the acts of kindness and thoughtfulness toward one another were on display daily in many ways.

One of my favorite stories involved Kadisha and Jaylani, an immigrant couple from Somalia. My friend George called me to ask if we could hire the couple who'd just moved about a mile from our facility. We'd been looking for a full-time custodian. Since neither Kadisha nor Jaylani spoke English yet, we figured cleaning would be the best starting point for them and hired them both. They were to come in after 5:00 p.m. each day to clean the office and common areas first, and later, after production had ended for the day, move on to clean the factory.

A few days into their employ, we learned that Jaylani and Kadisha had five small children. Rain or shine, they walked to LetterLogic with all five children in tow. One of them was an infant and the oldest was seven years old. Can you imagine walking a mile to and from work each day with five children? I couldn't.

I approached the leadership team with an idea to buy the couple a solid used car and pay their insurance for the first year, and they agreed. It would be a gift from the company, but we invited everyone to contribute if they wanted to, thereby making it a family affair. One of the employees scoured the county for a dependable car and eventually purchased an older-model Toyota Corolla.

The next week, we held our monthly employee meeting with Jaylani and Kadisha in attendance. We told them we had a gift to welcome them to Nashville and handed them a small gift-wrapped box. When Kadisha tore off the wrapping of the box to find a set of car keys, she acted like they'd won a million dollars. She leapt high into the air and was screaming with joy! They were completely overwhelmed with gratitude.

We led them out to the loading dock where the car was hidden. I had to cry when I saw the car. Our team had scrubbed, waxed, and polished the car and wrapped a giant bow around it. The best part was that everyone had gotten caught up in the gift: They'd gone above and beyond, without my knowing. The car trunk was loaded with extra gifts: clothing for the children, household items, diapers, strollers, and car seats. They embraced

Jaylani and Kadisha as part of the family and absolutely exemplified our family culture in the process.

Then there's the story of Michael Golden, which started with his brother, Will Golden. Will was a system administrator. He kept all the computers running and synchronizing. He had a great personality and literally a bounce in his step. He was a perfect coworker. We were so happy with him that when we learned he had a twin, there was no hesitation in hiring his brother, Michael.

Michael's skill and work ethic were not a surprise. We knew what to expect because his twin was so exemplary. What did bewilder us, though, was how quiet Michael was. He spoke only when necessary and did not socialize with us at all. He was the complete opposite of his outgoing brother. He'd been with us for a few weeks when his supervisor came to me to talk about him.

> "He was living proof that kindness and generosity beget kindness and generosity."

It turned out that Michael was a hockey player. A few months before we hired him, he'd lost his front teeth in a hockey match. Now it all made sense. The reason Michael wasn't as smiley and effervescent as his twin was because a few of his front teeth were missing. He didn't have dental insurance and was saving money to have his smile repaired. His supervisor asked if the company would help. Ten minutes later, he was headed back to the IT department with a check in his hand, a gift to take care of Michael's smile.

The hero in this story was the supervisor, a caring, empathetic leader who was looking out for his new family member. He was living proof that kindness and generosity beget kindness and generosity. Michael got his groove back when he got his smile back. Now he's married with a houseful of kids. Oh, and he went on to become the leader of the entire IT department and was honored as Family Member of the Year (our coveted MVP award, given by the employees) a few years later.

As Nashville was growing into a hotbed for tech start-ups, Michael was highly sought after. Though other companies constantly tried to lure him away from us, he remained loyal and dedicated to his family of coworkers. He became the same empathetic, thoughtful leader that his supervisor had been for him.

I could share these stories all day, but one of the sweetest involves our two oldest employees, Frank, our receptionist, and Harvey, our custodian. The two men came from very different backgrounds. Frank's father was an executive with the Singer Corporation (sewing machines). He grew up in Medellín, Colombia, with a houseful of servants and attended private school. He can recite, verbatim, everything William Shakespeare ever wrote, and he's an avid astronomer who can identify and name every constellation.

Harvey grew up in Detroit, Michigan. He was a two-time Golden Gloves champion in the bantam-weight division. A true sports fanatic, Harvey worked for the Vanderbilt University baseball team before he joined LetterLogic. If you ever need to know anything about the Detroit Lions, don't Google it. Just call Harvey. He'll know. When Harvey and Frank first began working together at LetterLogic, they were not quite in sync. They had little in common, but they tolerated each other. A year later, things had changed.

Harvey and I were sharing lunch after one of his weekend trips to Detroit. He told me that he had talked to Frank on the phone during the long drive back to Nashville, which had kept him awake.

"What?" I asked. "You called Frank?"

"No," he replied. "Frank always worries about me when I travel. He makes me call him when I leave town and when I get there. Then I have to call him again before I leave Detroit. If I get a late start, he calls me every hour or so to make sure I'm okay."

Imagining the two of them chatting while Harvey drove back to Nashville made me so happy.

WHERE YOU CAN JUST BREATHE

So what happened? How did these two men from such disparate backgrounds with almost nothing in common grow so close? It was a result of empathy. Frank and Harvey realized they were in an environment where there was no jockeying for position, no one looking to tear you down. Harvey describes it as finally being in a place "where you can just breathe. Not always on the run or looking over your shoulder." That environment gave them the latitude to start observing and appreciating the other.

Frank quietly noticed the camaraderie Harvey developed among all the employees. He watched Harvey sternly admonish them when they needed it and a few minutes later engage in playful banter. Harvey, on the other hand, was stunned to see the young men from the IT and production departments clock out at the end of the day, gather in the lobby, and sit on the floor with all eyes glued on Frank. What was this all about? Frank read poetry to them; he shared his love of Shakespeare, and he talked about upcoming astronomical events.

When Frank lost his hearing aid, Harvey was the first to lead the search. When Harvey needed directions to a new destination, Frank was the one who wrote out detailed instructions. Their care and empathy for each other led to a deep respect and love for one another.

Harvey says it best: "Frank P. LaVarre is my best friend. The best friend you could ever ask for."

THE FAMILY ALBUM

While reading *Delivering Happiness*, the book by Zappos CEO Tony Hsieh, I found a new inspiration. For those who don't know of it, Zappos is an online shoe retailer famous for its culture. Hsieh devotes a section to describing the company's "Culture Book," a thick, hardcover book, published annually, that profiles every Zappos employee. How cool is that?

I asked my leadership team if we too could create a culture book as a way to recognize our own extraordinary people and culture. Elizabeth Geist, our vice president of Client Services, was enthusiastic about the idea and asked to spearhead the project. She is a gifted writer with a background in publishing. She enlisted the help of Carrie Sublett, our graphic designer, who is also a professional photographer. They worked quietly for months on the project and still kept up their very demanding regular jobs. Later, Charlotte Brinkley, an account manager, joined their creative team.

The first LetterLogic Family Album was published in 2011. It beautifully encapsulated who we were as a company and paid homage to each individual. Every employee had their own profile page with photos of their families, their hobbies and interests, quotes from coworkers about them, and a paragraph about what the company meant to them.

My favorite part of that first Family Album was the superlatives section that Elizabeth and Carrie created for each person. They exemplified our closeness with great wit and affection. They're inside jokes, but that's what made them so funny. Some of them included:

- Most likely to be heard over a jet engine
- Most likely to crowd-surf with Ke$ha
- Most likely to bring a date *on* a date
- Least likely to be seen in the building

Even now, years later, those superlatives still resonate with anyone who was employed by LetterLogic at that time. They laugh out loud and know exactly who we were talking about, just the way you know all the funny quirks and attributes of your favorite cousins.

The LetterLogic Family Album was released annually at our year-end party. I couldn't wait to find a few hours to sneak off alone to go over every photograph and every page, laughing and crying. Better than anything else, the Family Albums captured the essence of who we were. I cherish my copies and I hope everyone else does too.

TAKEAWAY BOX:

Kindness and compassion are contagious.
Spread the love!

Third Course

ENTREES:
THE HOUSE SPECIALS

8

Our Signature Dish
Major in the Majors

"When your work speaks for itself, don't interrupt."

–Henry J. Kaiser

INGREDIENTS:

FOCUS.

Like all companies, at one point in our history, LetterLogic ran into some serious difficulties, and I began searching for the right person to help us get back on track. I was introduced to Brad Stevens at that time. He is a brilliant businessman and consultant, and his involvement with LetterLogic was pivotal to our success. What he brought to the company wasn't complicated or sophisticated, and it didn't result in a two-hundred-page consultancy report. He brought us a simple directive: Major in the Majors, which was a slogan influenced by Steven Covey's advice to "stop majoring in the minors."

At the time I met Brad, I'd already interviewed over thirty candidates. He was different—he didn't try to sell me on why I should hire him. Instead, he interviewed *me* to determine if we were a good fit. He was open and direct about his weaknesses, and further, he insisted that I would have to accept those weaknesses—as he was not interested in getting better in those areas. In fact, he wanted assurances that the company needed and wanted him for his *strength*: which was to affect change quickly. Because Brad had an impressive track record of helping companies, large and small, pinpoint problem areas and take corrective action swiftly, his typical engagement period was eighteen month or less, so we needed to use his time wisely. Thankfully, he agreed to take us on.

Taking Brad's counsel seriously, we focused on the company's strengths and used the leadership team's strengths to refocus. We pushed aside everything that didn't play to those strengths, and we adopted Brad's mantra: Major in the majors. Though I hadn't exactly used his "major in the majors" term, historically I had done just that. I had constantly eliminated distractions and focused on just a few things. That strategy had been part of our success. Until something changed: I had started to doubt my leadership and ignore my gut instincts. I got carried away with trying to become something I wasn't and to make the company something it couldn't be. And that is what got us into the big mess that made me seek out Brad.

DIRECT MAIL VERSUS TRANSACTIONAL MAIL

Here's the backstory on how we got into hot water. Whenever I described the service LetterLogic provided, it never failed. The person said, "Oh, you're in the direct mail business." We absolutely were *not* in the direct mail business, and if I had a dollar for every time I explained the difference to someone, I'd have a pile of cash to show you.

Let me explain the difference. Direct mail (aka "junk mail") is generally used for advertising purposes or promotional campaigns. Even in today's digital world, direct mail is still a good marketing channel because the response rates are decent and the cost is relatively low. Direct mail may be sent by what the USPS calls "standard mail," or "marketing mail," which is often referred to as third-class or bulk rate mail (though that is a misnomer).

Companies that use direct mail—let's say a postcard size advertisement—must first design and print the cards. Then the cards are delivered to a mailing company with the mailing list. The mailing company then prints the "variable data" (name and address of the recipient) on the piece and mails it. With the latest technologies in place, the entire project, including the graphics and variable data, can all be done by one company, and with one machine.

Even if everything about the project is perfect, which means that the colors are clean and vivid and there aren't any print shop mistakes, the client receives a bill for the one-time postcard mailing. After paying the bill, the customer doesn't need the printing and fulfillment company until they want another ad mailed. It might be months . . . or it might be years. That's how the direct mail industry works.

LetterLogic's business was the printing and fulfillment of *transactional* documents only—not marketing or promotional materials. We dealt with statements, invoices, or requests for payment for services—documents that *must* be received and acted upon in modern society. I'm talking about doctor bills, hospital bills, utility bills—stuff you don't necessarily WANT to receive, but that you must. Do you see the difference between this type of mail and most of what floods your mailbox every day?

Recognizing that transactional mail is more important than marketing mail, federal law requires that transactional documents *must* be mailed first class. Standard mail is not allowed for such items. Further, a mailing company that processes both standard mail *and* first-class mail must maintain separate processes for each, with entirely separate handling and reporting requirements.

Another important difference between direct mail and LetterLogic's service was the frequency with which we received customer data files. Though there was significant IT work and account setup to be done before the first statement was mailed for a new customer, once an account was set up and active, our customers sent us a data file daily—not every so often. Every day. Every week. Every month. Every year.

In fact, our first client back in 2002 sent about thirty thousand statements a month for us to process. When I sold the company fourteen years later, they were still sending the same volume, and we used the same interface we had developed for them at the onset (with several updates, of course). The recurring revenue that resulted was a consistent $20,000 a month, every month, for more than 168 months. That's over $3.3 million.

"... because we only did one thing, we became very, very good at it."

Had we been in the direct mail business and done an ad campaign for the same customer, it might have been months or years before they chose to do another. We would have needed to start fresh with new art and a new layout for every new campaign. But since we produced mail for them that was crucial to their revenue cycle, we were a "must"—an automatic.

Because I was fully aware of direct mail's challenges, I determined LetterLogic would focus exclusively on transactional, or first-class mail. From a business model standpoint, I chose to focus only on mail with *perennially recurring revenue potential*. I deliberately chose not to process any direct mail.

OUR EYES WERE BIGGER THAN OUR STOMACHS

Inevitably, as we added team members, especially in sales or leadership, the conversation around direct mail resurfaced. They suggested we were missing the boat because we could mail so many other things for our existing customers that we weren't. The logic seemed sound. Since we already mailed their statements, why not mail their newsletters, their annual reports, their brochures, and their checks too?

There were many reasons why we shouldn't have. The equipment to print statements is different from the equipment that prints ad slicks, postcards, brochures, or business cards. So we would need to have different equipment for those functions. As such, the workflow would be different for each function. We'd need more production employees with different skill sets. And we'd need a system to keep the first-class mail separate from the standard mail. All those processes required more equipment, many more people, and much more space—all of which meant we'd need a heck of a lot more money.

By majoring in the majors, which meant sticking to the print and fulfillment of transactional documents only, we had used less space, had fewer vendors and salespeople, and maintained a streamlined process. We had all that—and recurring revenue! For years! And because we only did one thing, we became very, very good at it. It allowed us to be the best in our industry.

Just as I had with my decision to deal only with transactional mail, I maintained my stance on focusing our efforts specifically on the healthcare industry. Healthcare was the world I knew, and I still had good relationships in the industry from when I sold services for my previous employer. But there were other compelling reasons.

I was keenly aware of unique challenges in the healthcare revenue cycle world. In the late 1990s, amid concerns that digitization would wreak havoc on the USPS, perhaps even force it out of business, I predicted that the healthcare industry would face its own peculiar set of needs and circumstances in that regard. The industry's challenges would make it a late adopter of electronic mail, and there was a large segment of the patient population that would always be resistant to electronic billing. I took an educated risk that this niche , the printing and mailing of patient bills, would be relatively safe for the next decade or so. I saw an opportunity to position LetterLogic to have compelling market distinctions and to effectively compete—even against the Goliaths that were already playing in that space.

However, though I wanted to continue our healthcare industry focus, people inside and outside the company were steadily pushing me to expand our offerings to other business types. The suggestions ranged from the financial industry—printing statements for credit unions and banks—to billing statements for utilities and telecom industries . . . and the home security monitoring business . . . and student loans . . . and hunting and fishing license renewals. See where this was going? Others saw business opportunities everywhere they looked. Though I occasionally investigated the market potential of another vertical, I chose to stay in the lane that belonged to the healthcare industry revenue cycle. *Right up until I didn't.* Until I got seduced into branching out, just a little.

For years, we'd been trying to get in the door at Vanderbilt University Medical Center. They sat there, just a mile from our facility, with about 150,000 statements a month to be mailed. They'd be a great mid-to-large size account. It aggravated me that we could win the business of hospitals in Texas, California, and Massachusetts, but we couldn't even get an appointment to present to Vanderbilt, right in our own backyard. Then one day, we got a call from Vanderbilt University (which is separate from the Medical Center). They asked us to print and mail their payroll checks and accounts payable checks. The door to Vanderbilt seemed to be opening. We were excited.

After some investigation, the excitement waned. I personally believed that bringing on non-healthcare business would be a mistake for a host of reasons, like those I mentioned previously. To start with, the printing equipment we owned and operated was not designed for printing checks. Check printing requires a process called magnetic ink character recognition (MICR), a special formulation of ink that prints a series of barcodes at the bottom of the check to aid in the prevention of fraud and abuse in banking. Since we didn't own a MICR printer, we'd need to get one. But if that printer was out of operation for repairs or routine maintenance, we wouldn't be able to service the customer, which meant we'd need at least *two* MICR printers. And because checks can be stolen and misused, check stock and the equipment that produces checks must be kept in a separate, secure location with cameras to monitor throughout. We'd also be required to have a federal certification to process checks.

To process checks for this one entity, we'd have to buy new equipment; create a new workflow; enclose, lock, and monitor a section of our facility; and specifically train individuals for just one client. Because we'd never done this type of business, we weren't sure how to price it. For all these reasons, I recommended we walk away from the opportunity.

Others in the company were convinced we should take the business. They believed it was the entree we needed to Vanderbilt University Medical Center. Even though it was with a totally different division of Vanderbilt, they shared a campus and a few key executives. Those in favor of the idea suggested we leverage the university business to get the medical center business after we dazzled them with our service. And then there was the "flagship account" caché effect. Really—what business wouldn't want to list Vanderbilt as a client?

After much discussion and internal haggling, I reluctantly agreed to allow the team to move forward. My caveat was that if we won the business, we would lease the MICR printers on a click-charge basis. That meant we would pay a modest lease payment *plus* a fee for each image (or "click") created by the printers to cover the cost of the ink, toner, and maintenance. If our new line of business didn't work out, at least we wouldn't be stuck with expensive equipment we couldn't use.

> " ... We won the business. And we almost lost our shirts."

As fate would have it, we won the business. And we almost lost our shirts. We underestimated how disruptive this single new client would be to our regular workflow. We established the expectation that we could deliver the same high level of service we were known for. After all, this was just "printing and fulfillment," right? Wrong. Very wrong.

Up until this time, 100 percent of our daily workload was subject to the same protocol: Each file was processed and printed within twenty-four hours of receipt of client data, and then every envelope was delivered to the USPS by 7:00 p.m. However, our new client wanted to send the data to us at midnight and have the checks processed, printed, inserted *but not mailed*! Instead of mailing the checks, we were to package them for the client to pick up by 6:00 a.m. (Remember, our sole business was in printing *and mailing* documents.) In addition to needing a separate, unique workflow with a dedicated secure space and dedicated handlers, we also had only six hours to complete the work, which made the one-off client a priority above everyone else.

Frankly, on an ideal day, six hours would have been sufficient. But when is there ever an ideal day in a production facility (or most companies, for that matter)? Almost never. We had set ourselves up for failure, and we set the client up for constant disappointment. We damaged our reputation and our brand by getting out of our lane and doing work that did not fit our workflow. To add insult to injury, we had also dramatically underestimated the cost. There was no way to break even; we lost money on every check we printed.

We immediately went into damage control mode. First, we met with the client to confess our miscalculations regarding pricing and timing. We told them it would be best if they chose another vendor but that we would continue to service them until a smooth transition could be made. To our surprise, they said they wanted to stay with us and were willing to pay us more! Next, we told them how the timing requirement affected our daily workflow and asked them to make adjustments. They did.

Vanderbilt University used LetterLogic for its check printing and fulfillment (but nothing more) for several years after our painful admission. In retrospect, we never should have started the work to begin with. We rationalized taking the business based on so many IFs:

- "IF we get this business, we can get the healthcare business too."

  We didn't.

- "IF we buy this equipment and perfect our check-printing process, we can add more check-printing business from other clients."

  We didn't.

- "IF we get Vanderbilt's business, won't it be so great and powerful to have them as a client for references?"

We didn't, simply because we never gave them the same level of service we gave to our other clients. *Their needs were not in line with our strengths,* and therefore, we were not comfortable using them as a reference. The point of this story is that I had stopped "majoring in the majors." I had strayed from our signature dishes. Worse, I allowed self-doubt to override my gut instincts (and industry experience) that had told me not to take on work that was outside our tried and true repertoire of dishes.

$$\vdash \mathbb{T} \dashv$$

Hindsight is 20/20. At least I learned a lesson and never had to learn it again, right? Wrong.

When I founded LetterLogic, I was acutely aware of the impact e-commerce was going to have on the industry. Even so, I made the decision to be a paper-based business, and I intentionally chose not to develop or buy the technology to send statements electronically. Instead, I was committed to us being the best paper-based vendor in the industry and to partner with the best-in-class e-commerce vendors to take care of our clients.

My logic was sound. If we'd been servicing almost any other industry, we'd likely have had to pursue electronic commerce options sooner. As I mentioned earlier, indications were that the healthcare industry would be a late adopter, and utilization rate by the patient population would be low too. Hospitals were buying e-commerce technology later than other industries, and when they did, many patients still wanted to receive a paper bill.

My assumption was that because healthcare billing is so complex and confusing, many patients (myself included) wanted to gather all the paper bills from their different providers and compare them with the reams of paper we get from the insurance company before we decide what we owe and who to pay. Further, since most medical incidents are a one-time occurrence, I guessed that patients would be less likely to go online to create a profile for payment.

But in reality, hospitals were becoming increasingly competitive. They needed every possible advantage to build patient loyalty. It was just good business to offer the patient multiple billing and payment options, and that included online. So the hospitals began clamoring for e-commerce options. In fact, most requests for proposals (RFPs) required e-commerce to be a fundamental. Like everyone else in the business, LetterLogic had to respond to this requirement.

By that time, we had succeeded in developing a short list of good vendors we could partner with for electronic statements and sophisticated payment options. None of the vendors had *everything* a client would ask for, but we could meld together an acceptable solution for each client (with a small revenue share to us) from these e-commerce partners. This agnostic approach allowed us to be responsive to RFPs and to tailor a solution for each opportunity. The downside was that each of these vendors/partners needed us to create a custom interface through which we could pass the data back and forth. With every new partner, we were investing a ton of money and time for integration.

I was receiving pressure from the sales team to buy or build our own solution; one that would address every conceivable e-commerce request a hospital might throw our way. The technology wish list was constantly growing. I was blinded by the fear of missing out (FOMO) and didn't want to be left behind in our industry. I succumbed to internal and external pressures and hired a CTO to assemble and lead a technology team to build the best e-commerce engine in the business.

To be honest, I'm not tech-savvy, and I had no way to monitor his activity or progress. And to be fair, I didn't give him a succinct plan or clear outcome expectations. I just gave him free rein and told him to "build it"—a new technology company that I thought would complement our business. I turned my attention away from him and focused on selling the products we didn't have. I secured the domain name and began the trademarking process. I hired outside firms to help flesh out the needs for the new entity.

Meanwhile, back in our IT department, the free rein I had given to the CTO turned into a hiring frenzy. In just a few months, we ballooned from fifty to sixty-four employees, from junior developers and data analysts to project managers and highly trained code writers. We hired them so quickly there was no way to vet their skill level or their culture fit. Heck, there was no place for them to sit! My priority quickly shifted to renting more space to house the new people and then outfitting the space to be cool enough for the new techies. Immediately, we added 3,000 square feet of office space.

There was no time to train all the new hires—even on the basics of our industry. Because the data we received and printed was HIPAA protected, with privacy mandates and timing sensitivities, we couldn't just set these individuals free to work and figure it out on their own. So they sat and waited for us to get our act together and give them some guidance and leadership. That never came.

Spending was out of control. The addition of the new employees and office space quickly took a toll. We'd been profitable for years, but suddenly the profits were dwindling; each month saw them sinking lower and lower. And then we had two months of back-to-back losses. When the projected delivery date for the e-commerce solution was repeatedly pushed further out into the future, I reasoned, "You've gotta spend money to make money." We were in the midst of this hell when I determined I'd put the wrong person in charge of the new enterprise, and I terminated his employment.

I had a pretty big mess on my hands—a huge, expensive department with the wrong leader was now without a leader. And we were losing money. That meant no profit share, and *that* killed me. The long-standing loyal employees suffered due to my failure to maintain our focus on our core competency.

All sorts of experts may tell you to diversify, to add multiple products and service lines. And while that might be good advice in some industries, or at a certain point in a company's growth, I've seen it be the very reason many entrepreneurs fail. One of my friends did so well in one vertical of the printing business that he decided to add five more. His attention was quickly diluted; he lost focus, and ultimately had to sell the best of the five to avoid losing his home. There are thousands of such stories, where entrepreneurs got distracted, just as I did, and lost their shirts as a result.

STICK TO YOUR SIGNATURE DISH

That's when Brad Stevens came on the scene. Within his first two weeks, Brad shared his observation that we weren't "majoring in the majors." He believed we'd gotten dramatically off course and were heading toward a black hole if I didn't lead us back to our core business.

Brad was direct. He said, "You've spent a ton of money trying to become a tech company, and you can spend millions more without catching up to where the technology is today. You have turned away from what made your company successful—being the very best in the paper-statement business. In essence, you're trying too hard to be something you're not. Embrace who you are! Notice that your competitors are in this boat alongside you. They're struggling and jostling for position too. But since they've never been great at delivering a perfect paper product, the distraction of the e-commerce business will likely cause them to get even worse. If you refocus on being the best at your core business, printing and mailing, you'll have a better chance of surviving the industry change and becoming the undisputed winner."

Brad was right.

The best example of what happens when a business chooses to major in the majors or stick to their signature dish is Southwest Airlines.[5] Full disclosure: I always had a business crush on Southwest co-founder Herb Kelleher. When Herb started the airline, he made a few commonsense—but oh-so-genius—moves:

1. He made the decision to buy one airplane model only. His competitors had lots of aircraft, but Southwest had only the Boeing 737. Why? Because with only one airplane model, they only had to stock one kind of parts. And every mechanic would be fully trained to work on every plane. And every flight crew would know every plane. But what if a flight wasn't fully booked and a much smaller plane was needed instead of the 737 . . . When was the last time you were on a Southwest flight that wasn't full?

2. Instead of trying to be everything to everybody, Southwest focused on being the low-cost provider. That meant no food; just peanuts. That meant no assigned seats; just first-come, first-serve boarding.

3. Southwest operates on a point-to-point basis. So the flight crew takes the plane from Raleigh to Nashville, unloads and reloads, and in thirty minutes or so is heading back to Raleigh. In this way, they attract loyal business travelers commuting for work.

---

5   When I started LetterLogic, I only went after clients in cities with direct Southwest flights. If Southwest didn't fly there, we didn't pursue business there. If Southwest was there, we could get cheap flights and had no need to stay in hotels, which kept our selling expense as low as possible. Our salespeople loved the free companion pass and the rapid rewards they got to keep for their own personal use.

There are a dozen other smart practices that led Southwest to almost forty consecutive years of profitability. At the core, though, they followed a very basic, "boring" plan, and yet a plan that was elegant in its honesty and simplicity. *They knew who they were and who they wanted to attract as loyal clients.* When the other airlines struggled financially, Southwest kept chugging along, making money and building their loyal base.

So how did LetterLogic get back to our signature dish? First off, the new tech spinoff had to go, and I had to go back to my original strategy.

Under Brad's direction, we stopped the development of the e-commerce model. It was a smart financial decision. I was already lamenting the outrageous expense for the IT talent we'd hired when I learned that we also had to be certified for payment card industry data security standard (PCI-DSS) compliance—a process that would add an estimated $1 million in annual fees on top of all the other expenses. Enough! We knew what our loyal customers wanted, and we went back to our original concept of partnering with companies that had already built the e-commerce process and whose business models already included the compliance expense.

We told all the new people we had hired that we were not building an e-commerce platform after all. Instead, we were honest about our plans to build interfaces to integrate the technology built by strategic partners. A few of our highest-paid newcomers were contract workers, and when their contracts expired, they moved on. When the junior developers learned they wouldn't be doing the sexy work of creating software, they left to find work that was more inspiring to them. Those who were happy to focus on account maintenance and integration work stayed, and before too long, the IT department had self-corrected. It was back to a manageable, well-trained, engaged group of eight to ten people. The impact on the bottom line was positive and immediate.

Then we narrowed our e-commerce partnerships to just two. We stopped trying to have every feature for every customer. We stopped our knee-jerk reactions and stopped saying yes to everything a customer could dream of wanting.

Once we determined we would no longer be on the bleeding edge of expensive technology, Kennon Askew, our vice president of Business Development, wisely insisted we become thought leaders. Instead of stepping in as our clients' e-commerce service provider, we helped them find practical, innovative solutions and connected them with good partners. We educated them. We shared our research and data with them about what worked and what didn't for patient engagement and revenue improvement.

Did this stance halt our growth? Did it negatively affect our top line growth? Not at all. We continued to grow, and we continued our stint as an Inc. 5000 company (*Inc.* magazine's list of the fastest-growing privately held businesses in the nation) for *ten consecutive years*. And it was the beginning of an eighteen-month period where we quadrupled our profit.

During his tenure, Brad quietly and humbly coached and mentored us. Using his business savvy, we lived by a one-page strategic plan. When I say we "lived" by it, I mean that each month Brad laminated and distributed this single page to the leadership team. We knew that if a project wasn't on that laminated sheet, we wouldn't waste time talking about it. We acquired laser-sharp focus. He taught us to think like him, to remove distractions and work to our strengths—to major in the majors.

If I could clone Brad, I'd sell him to all of you and make a bazillion dollars. But if you take his advice and simply spend the bulk of your time on things that make the biggest impact to your business, you'll be on your way to majoring in the majors.

WHAT YOUR LOYAL CUSTOMERS COME BACK FOR

But how does the practice of sticking to that perfect signature dish we were known for relate to empathy? If you'd been around during the tumultuous months when we feverishly added new people, you would know. You'd have seen and felt the negative affect on our culture and on our team members' quality of life. I confused them by giving them conflicting priorities and chasing the latest trends. I dangled the idea of new dishes (products) we could make and then hired strangers (not even my own staff members) to do that exciting new work. I publicly touted that we were a close-knit family, yet I adopted new members so quickly that we didn't have time to even welcome them properly. This isn't what empathy looks like.

To put everything into perspective, can you imagine the pain and havoc you'd wreak if you suddenly started bringing newly adopted children into your home while your own children were clamoring for your affection? And then what if you told them the whole family was moving to a new neighborhood—to a house that hadn't even been built yet? It was a crazy time, and I did not behave in a way that was consistent with our values, and it certainly wasn't the empathic culture I had so carefully cultivated.

TAKEAWAY BOX:
Do one thing. Do it really, really well, and you'll succeed.

9

Pass the Salt, Please
Direct, Empathetic Communication

"Let your words always be gracious, seasoned with salt . . ."

−Colossians 4:6

INGREDIENTS:

DIRECTNESS, THOUGHTFULNESS, AND TACT.

My father, Harold Bryan Stewart, Jr., passed away in March 2016 at the age of eighty. For several months, he'd had bouts of weakness, and he fell occasionally for no obvious reason. He'd seen several doctors, but by the time he was diagnosed with bile duct cancer, it had metastasized to his brain. The brain tumors were causing the falls. Though he died only a few short months after the diagnosis, it was enough time for me to have several long conversations with him, including the tough ones about funeral arrangements and how we planned to make him comfortable during the last few weeks. Those tough conversations were a privilege, because I had a special relationship with Dad that allowed me to give him the honest, direct feedback he didn't get from anyone else.

My father was dogmatic and unbalanced. Most people who knew him well and loved him would agree with that assessment. In many ways, he was a dictator: sometimes a benevolent one and sometimes a harsh one. He gave orders to everyone around him—from his employees to his wife and children. Most of the time, we all jumped immediately to follow his commands. He was a complicated man. He was a stocky 5'10" with broad shoulders, curly hair (what was left of it after raising seven children), and hazel eyes. He was handsome enough to be named "Best Looking" in his high school yearbook and had his own unique brand of charm. He was smart and adventurous and loved to talk with strangers. With Dad, *no one* was a stranger.

When he was sixteen, much to the displeasure of his Methodist family, he began studying the Bible with Jehovah's Witnesses. He converted just four years later at age twenty. He pursued his new faith like he did everything else that interested him—at full tilt with no reservations. For the next sixty years, Dad put his faith ahead of everything else. Everything.

Dad loved his wife and family, but in my opinion, he mistreated both. As I child, I marveled at how he would preach about kindness and then treat Mom so badly. He believed he was almost always right and could not abide anyone who disagreed with him. He called them "jackasses" (the only "bad language" I ever heard from him), "ignoramuses," and most often, "boneheads."

Our special bond started when I was twelve, over the course of an hour—an hour I will never forget. It forever changed the dynamic of our relationship and served as a launching point every time I feared a tough and necessary conversation.

The handbook or primer for Jehovah's Witnesses is called *The Truth That Leads to Eternal Life*. It became known as "The Truth Book" and was used to teach the basics of Christian behavior and Jehovah's Witness doctrine to new converts. It's one of the best-selling books of all time, and most Witnesses know it inside and out, cover-to-cover, Dad included.

The Truth Book was just as much a part of my childhood as the L-shaped kitchen in our house. The sink and cabinets were on the long side of the L, and the oven and fridge were on the short side. The other half of the kitchen held a large table with a row of chairs on one side and a custom-made bench along the wall on the other—enough room to accommodate our family of nine and a few visitors from time to time. On a typical night, all of us—Dad, Mom, and my six siblings and I—had supper together at that table. Each meal began with a brief discussion of a Bible text from the Jehovah's Witnesses Yearbook, followed by a prayer.

On one particular night, following the text discussion, Dad spoke sharply down to Mom. That wasn't unusual; it was the norm. As was also common, the rest of us stopped talking and finished dinner solemnly. After the girls washed the dishes and we all escaped to our bedrooms, I pulled out *The Truth Book.* I found the chapter entitled "How to Have a Happy Family Life." I thought about how Dad treated Mom in contrast to how *The Truth Book* said a husband should treat his wife. He was supposed to treat her with respect and kindness. He was supposed to love her and cherish her. Instead, he treated her harshly, constantly belittling her and telling her to "hold her tongue." I was just a twelve-year-old girl, but I couldn't stand by any longer and watch it happen. I had to speak up.

Knowing that the Bible and Jehovah's Witness literature were the only things Dad would listen to, I crept from my bedroom down the black iron spiral staircase and into the living room. I found Dad lounging in his green vinyl La-Z-Boy recliner, reading the latest issue of *The Watchtower* (the magazine for Jehovah's Witnesses). With great fear, I approached him, *The Truth Book* in hand. In a small, quivering voice, I asked him, "Daddy, can I read something to you?" He nodded.

I began reading the one paragraph I wanted him to hear, and he came totally unglued. He kicked down the footrest and sat upright in his recliner.

He yelled, "I know that book better than anyone!" I dropped the book on the floor and ran back up the stairs, peeing in my pants as I ran, so terrified was I of his anger and hot temper. I fell sobbing into my bedroom and dissolved into a puddle of tears. There was no other sound in the house.

Fifteen minutes passed, and I was heading to the bathtub when I heard my father call out in a weary voice, "Sher, come back down here." For the second time that night, I crept down the stairs to face him. He quietly handed me *The Truth Book* and said, "Please, read to me what you wanted to read to me." I did. I cried in fear and relief with every word, my voice quivering and my hands shaking, but I read it to him, tears streaming down my face. When I finished, I looked up, and my dad's head was hanging down. There was total quiet in the room—only the sound of the fire crackling in the woodstove. After a few seconds of silence that seemed like hours, I asked, "Can I go now?" He nodded and uttered a sentence that changed our relationship: "You're a smart youngin."

The passage I read to him can be paraphrased as follows:

The husband is to take the lead in the home, but this does not authorize him to be a harsh or cruel ruler. Husbands shall not be overly demanding of their wives, but will handle family affairs in a way that refreshes everyone concerned. When a husband does this, he helps bring about a spirit of understanding and security in the home.

Dad and I never spoke of that evening again. Most of my siblings and my mom didn't know about it until after his death. But I knew. And he knew. And from that point on, Dad treated me differently. I don't mean that he no longer yelled at me or that he suddenly became a different man. I mean only that a subtle change occurred in how he saw me. He began to respect me and listen to me. This marked a decades-long struggle to be kinder and gentler and to show affection and appreciation to Mom.

Many years later, when I was being honored as a "Woman of Influence," someone asked me, "When was the first time you knew you had the power to influence?" Immediately I thought of that conversation with Dad. I also recalled that I had carefully planned my approach and my words for the situation. If I'd confronted him at the table in front of everyone, or if I'd yelled back at him in the moment, or if I'd not referenced an authority that *he* would have listened to, everything would likely have been different. I knew Dad well enough to know I had to present any counsel from an authority he respected. In that way, I wasn't an impudent child challenging him; I was sharing words from a passage that he knew well and had publicly touted. It would be hard for him to fault the source.

My empathy for Mom—and for Dad—led to my boldness and thoughtfulness in the situation. Empathy for Mom: of course! *But empathy for my dad?* He was being a tyrant. Why should I have empathy for him? I had reason to believe that my father's childhood had been devoid of affection. Indeed, his father was known to be cruel. So I absolutely had compassion and empathy for him. But there were other reasons.

Even as a little girl, I knew how hard it must have been to earn a living for such a large family. I knew how hard he worked. I saw him. I remembered the special occasions when he took us all out to dinner at the Cardinal Restaurant in Boone, North Carolina. I marveled at him—the person at the rear of that cafeteria line, picking up the tab for the nine of us—and I recall being very grateful for his willingness to treat us to a dinner out. My siblings felt it too. I recall the nine of us crammed into the VW bus on the way home. One of us started with "Thank you for taking us out, Daddy" and then the echo of gratitude from the others followed.

PASS THE SALT—AND THE EMPATHY

You may be wondering what this particular story has to do with my overall theme of bringing empathy to work. How can you use empathy to provide your employees with performance feedback or have the humility to accept performance feedback from *them* when you need it? The Bible tells us "let your speech be always with grace, seasoned with salt, that you may know how you ought to answer every man." I'm not a likely source of Bible quotations, but this one has always stuck with me. Although there are varying interpretations of this verse, I take it to mean that I could make my message more palatable by choosing my words carefully. If you want to make any message more palatable or meaningful for an individual, you must start by knowing that person well—and having that person know *you* well too. It's only then that you can put yourself in the other person's shoes (and they in yours) and be able to speak with directness *and* kindness as you deliver your message.

Here's where my approach differs from that of most business coaches and esteemed authorities. Many of them advise you to give corrective feedback in a "sandwich" format. You start by praising the employee, then tell them something they need to work on, and close with praise. That might work for some people, but it just doesn't work for me, no matter which side of the table I'm sitting on.

> **"The most effective and compassionate way to deliver criticism is to be direct."**

If I were on the receiving end, I'd know that criticism was coming. I would brace for it, and I would be too distracted with anticipation to hear the positives—and the positives would be outweighed by the negatives anyway. When I'm on the critiquing side, I feel like a fraud if I start out with praise and then follow up with negative feedback. This tactic feels manipulative. The most effective and compassionate way to deliver criticism is to be direct.

A few months before Dad passed away, we sat side by side in his matching leather recliners. He told me I was the only person he felt he could talk with honestly about his mistakes and his regrets. It was at once a burden and a privilege to be his confidante. But that one night of fear and courage as a twelve-year-old taught me to see the value of facing tough situations and conversations head on, and that was a lesson that has helped me many times in business. Empathy for my mom is what made me take action and speak up to my dad in spite of my fear. I can channel that little girl today and recall her dread and anxiety when she felt compelled to confront an authority figure—her own father. I can also put myself in an employee's place when they are courageous enough to challenge my decisions or actions. Channeling the young me makes me more approachable and reasonable, so I can actually listen to what my employees have to say. [6]

BEING DIRECT WITH EMPLOYEES

I had to practice, practice, practice being direct with employees. At heart, I'm a softy and a people pleaser, so there were many times when I totally wimped out if I had to meet with an employee to talk about a mistake or performance weakness. I'd start to feel bad and water down the message or be overly sympathetic. Instead of using the situation to coach and correct, I'd send them out of my office with a hug. I wasn't doing them any favors because they didn't know if they'd been chastised or praised.

Eventually, I figured out how to deal with my weakness in this area. First, I reviewed all the facts of the situation or incident; then every note and document. Then I carefully drafted an outline to put structure to the scenario, as I understood it. After that, I reviewed the situation with a third party—the head of HR or one of my senior leaders—so that I could lay out my understanding of the facts. Finally, I shared what I planned to say to the employee and even rehearsed my responses to possible reactions or excuses.

Reviewing and rehearsing with a third party made me take responsibility for accurately knowing—and being able to articulate—the facts. If the third party let me know that more nuance or substance was needed, or that

---

6   In 2014, I met a successful entrepreneur, Michael Brody-Waite. His mantra was, "Always, always, be direct." The phrase was framed on several walls in his offices. I immediately copied Michael's behavior, and if you visited my office anytime after 2014, you would have seen that phrase handwritten on my whiteboard in large, bold letters. I looked at it every morning and meditated over it for a few minutes before every tough conversation I had to have.

I had overlooked something or was overreacting, I had time to alter my approach. At the very least, I got a good second opinion and a check on my rationale, which gave me the confidence I needed to proceed—regardless of what type of action was needed.

When the situation required a direct conversation with the employee, I asked the third party to be with me for HR compliance purposes, but more importantly, to hold *me* accountable. I couldn't wimp out. I had to follow through and do what I said I was going to do. Aside from modeling a compassionate way to deliver correction, this approach gave the third party confidence that I said what I meant and meant what I said. It built their faith in me as a leader. Sometimes the only corrective action I needed to take was just to let the person understand the impact of their actions. One particular incident comes to mind.

During one specific phase in our company history, we were making far too many mistakes. The primary source of the errors was one hardworking, brilliant programmer. In his defense, we were growing very quickly and we placed a lot of pressure on him to onboard new clients. Unfortunately, he made several seemingly small mistakes that ended up having serious consequences. He'd been open about the problems and quick to correct them, but he continued to make errors. And I wasn't able to make him understand how badly his errors affected the customers—and the company, as a result.

"When the programmer saw the clear cause and effect of his mistakes and the role he played in each, he changed his behavior and process."

One day, I was getting ready to call a customer to let them know about a significant mistake we'd made when it occurred to me to have the programmer listen in on the call. I didn't announce his presence to the customer; I only wanted him to hear the conversation.

With the customer on speakerphone, I went through the painful process of breaking the bad news. I shared all the pertinent details. The programmer heard firsthand the ripple effect of his seemingly small mistake.

He heard the anxiety in the customer's voice. He heard me laying bare the issues and my admission that it was due to human error. And he heard me tell the customer the steps we were taking to make it right, which included issuing a credit for the entire job valued at $7,000.

That was all it took. When the programmer saw the clear cause and effect of his mistakes and the role he played in each, he changed his behavior and process. Remember, including him in the discussion was not an effort to shame him in any way—the customer didn't even know he was listening in. It was just a very useful and productive way of being direct, and it got the results I was hoping for: He finally understood why he had to be more careful. In addition, his confidence in me as a leader was strengthened when he heard how direct I was with the customer about the problem. There was no sugarcoating.

I also admitted that it was *our* fault; not his. Ultimately, no matter where a mistake was made within the organization, as the CEO, I was responsible. I appointed the leadership team who hired and trained our staff, and I approved the processes they used. If there was a failure anywhere along the way, it was on me. My job was to make sure the employees knew that I had their backs—even when they made careless mistakes.

On another occasion, I had to terminate one of our senior leaders. Because of the security requirements in our industry, every termination necessitated an immediate change to the security codes for all doors. This meant that within minutes, as we notified employees of the new security codes, the entire company knew someone had resigned or been fired. In 95 percent of terminations, no one was surprised; they usually just wondered why it had taken so long. But in this situation, because the person was so senior and their misdeeds so hidden (even from me), as soon as they were escorted to the door and the door code changed, I called a mandatory company meeting.

If I hadn't tackled the person's termination immediately and head on, the staff would have been left guessing about what happened. And speculation doesn't help anyone. While carefully measuring my words to ensure I didn't violate any HR laws, I announced that the person was no longer with us because they displayed a disregard for our company values; their actions, if left unchecked, would have endangered everyone's livelihood.

My message was brief, and I allowed time for questions. It was a somber meeting, but dealing with the situation directly short-circuited the drama and gossip that might have ensued otherwise. Within fifteen minutes, everyone was back at their workstations, and we moved on, drama free.

My Good Traits—and My Bad Ones Too

Our employees knew my good traits and my bad ones too. They knew my hot buttons and they—better than anyone else in my life—knew where I needed to grow and learn. One unique, weird quality of mine is that I respond better to negative criticism than to praise. It's probably my "not good enough" complex that makes me doubt a person who delivers praise. If someone tells me where I fall short, I'm all ears.

Knowing myself well enough to know I could handle the heat, I periodically asked a diverse sampling of employees to evaluate my leadership performance. In those cases, I had them meet with a consultant who interviewed them, collected their feedback, and aggregated their responses to share with me anonymously. What a gift! It was humbling and inspiring to see my employees' thoughtful advice on how I could improve my interactions with them and how to be a better leader. If you haven't done this yet, I encourage you to give it a try. It's an eye-opening, affirming exercise.

BEING DIRECT WITH CUSTOMERS

From the beginning, I established clear expectations with our customers by telling them that though I believed we were the best patient-statement company in the business, we were bound to make mistakes from time to time. Before they signed a contract, I told them I could *guarantee* we would make mistakes, either in the first few weeks of our relationship or in year five. But I also assured them that when that day came, we would notify them as soon as we knew of any mistake. We would not sugarcoat or minimize the incident. Further, I promised I would personally deliver any bad news.

Years later, when we'd grown so much that I hadn't met most of our customers, I still made the call when there was a significant client problem. The call was important for a number of reasons:

- It totally and immediately de-escalated the situation. If anyone else had made the call, the customers were still likely to call me to make sure I knew what had happened and how upset they were. By preempting that call, I let them know we took the error seriously enough to get the CEO involved.

- It let my team know that I had their backs and that I would take responsibility for our mistakes without recrimination.

- It spoke volumes to the customer about our integrity as a company. In almost every situation, the mistake—and the way we handled it— only strengthened our relationship with them.

- It told my team that our mistakes, *their* mistakes, mattered a great deal to our customers; enough that the CEO herself insisted on being informed so that she could personally handle the customer communication.

Dealing with customer problems swiftly and directly prevented us from committing one of my biggest pet peeves in business—the "sorry for any inconvenience" brush-off. I absolutely hate it when a company uses that phrase to address a problem. Every new account manager at LetterLogic heard my diatribe about this, so I'm sharing it with you too:

- An "inconvenience" is when your plane arrives early and you have to wait for the gate agents to get the sky bridge ready.

- An "inconvenience" is when the grocery store runs out of cilantro the night you're making burritos, or when your spaghetti is not served al dente.

Get the point?

Most of our mistakes were due to simple human error. That means that somewhere along the way, at least one employee failed to do what they were supposed to do, and subsequently our customer was impacted. Because we were in the business to business (B2B) sector, when our customers were impacted, so were *their* customers. The ripple effect of a seemingly small mistake could impact tens of thousands of individuals at once. Calling a mistake an "inconvenience" or blaming it on a "glitch" or a "bug" is a total cop-out.

> "Most people can smell BS a mile away, and they'll run from the stench as soon as they can."

Being direct and taking full responsibility helped diffuse the customer's anger and frustration. Sometimes that meant admitting that someone had not been adequately trained or acknowledging a gap in the code we'd written. Sometimes it meant admitting to carelessness. Admit we were careless? Who does that? The truth is we can *all* be careless at times. No matter how good you are, or how diligent and conscientious, every now and then you screw up and miss an important step. This applies to everyone: to you, to me, to your customers, and to mine. People appreciate the truth, and no one wants to be bamboozled. Most people can smell BS a mile away, and they'll run from the stench as soon as they can.

When we made a mistake that necessitated a call to the customer, I insisted the client services manager let me know personally. I followed the same process as when an employee situation necessitated feedback. As soon as I learned of an incident, I set out to make sure I had the facts straight—which meant I didn't rely on the facts as they were told to me. It meant I dug into all the records and talked with everyone involved. It wasn't because I didn't trust my team to tell the truth or that I didn't trust their understanding of the situation. It was because I had to be able to understand the mistake well enough to clearly explain it to someone else. Then I placed a call directly to the highest-ranking person with whom we had a relationship within the customer's organization.

After the obligatory greeting, I told the customer I was calling with bad news. In the next sentence, I gave them a succinct description of what we'd done wrong. I told them *when* it happened, *how* it happened, *why* it happened, *how* we discovered the error, and *who* was affected—meaning how widespread the problem was. And finally, I told them how we intended to fix the problem and when it would be resolved. I gave them details. I told them the truth and answered their questions. I ended the call with the promise to email them a report of everything we'd just discussed: The who, what, why, how, and when. I also offered, when appropriate, to write a letter of explanation they could share with *their* customers if needed, stating that the mistake originated from us, the vendor. And I never, ever minimized the mistake as an "inconvenience."

The results always proved this approach was the right one. Customers understand human error; they have their own to contend with. The fact that I laid bare all the dirty details gave them *more* confidence in us, not less. I can't remember a single time when the customer was angry with me during one of those calls. Of course, they were disappointed with the mistake, but the honesty, directness, and timeliness totally mitigated the situation.

At the heart of all this directness, once again, was our policy to always put the employees ahead of everything else. How is laying bare a problem to a customer putting the employee first? When we researched a problem to determine the root cause and who had made the mistake, we weren't looking for someone to blame. We were trying to identify the weakness in our system or processes that made it possible for the person's mistake to be made and to go unchecked. We wanted to make sure the person saw the impact of the mistake and learned from it. The sooner we corrected the error, the quicker we could recover, make any necessary financial concessions to the customer, and get right back on the profitability train and those great profit share checks. Back to taking extraordinary care of the employees.

TAKEAWAY BOX:

It's disrespectful to BS your way through a difficult conversation. Be kind. Be honest.

10

An Open Kitchen
Authenticity on Display

"A lack of transparency results in distrust and a deep sense of insecurity."

–Dalai Lama

INGREDIENTS:

TRANSPARENCY.

As you've likely noticed by now, a basic tenet of life at LetterLogic was that we were family. This concept was central to our culture, and it was expected that we treat each other with the same respect and kindness that we would show our own family members. But knowing how dysfunctional many families are, we modified our model and encouraged everyone to treat one another as they'd treat their favorite cousin. We could all live with that.

Our values statement reflected our family-like culture:

We are a family of unique individuals who care deeply about each other and our clients. We are successful because we are empowered, and we use our power to make LetterLogic better.

I make a difference because:

- *I Care*
- *I Take Responsibility*
- *I Embrace Change*
- *I Make Work Fun*

While our values statement clearly broadcast our intent as a group, it just as clearly put the responsibility on the individual—on every individual.

During our monthly company meetings, we recognized and honored those who best lived our values—values that captured the essence of who we were as a family. We created a ritual of shutting down operations for a few hours every month to have lunch together. The location changed throughout the years as we continued to grow and add "family members," but the practice never changed.

At first, the company lunch consisted of a couple of pizzas, and then it was boxed lunches. For the last several years, when our budget was bigger, we had our lunches catered by local restaurants. All the food was set up out on the factory floor, buffet-style, on a massive sage-green tiled bar we bought from the Habitat Re-Store for just that purpose. At about twelve feet long and thirty inches wide, we could fit a lot of fried chicken and potato salad on that bar! While the caterers unpacked and arranged the food, several of us pitched in to set up, putting out tables and chairs, spreading tablecloths, filling cups with ice, and pouring iced tea. Everyone was eager to help and looked forward to the meeting.

Our meetings began when everyone was settled with their first plate of food. We started with the same announcements you'd expect at a typical family reunion—engagements, weddings, new babies on the way, graduations, vacation plans. We always made time to welcome the newest employees in our LetterLogic family. Following the opening announcements, each department provided an update on the challenges and triumphs they had experienced in the last thirty days. Failing equipment? The efficiency of new equipment? A problem customer? A new customer who temporarily consumed a lot of attention? A change in our health insurance coverage? We talked about whatever might impact the daily lives of our family members and answered any questions.

OPEN-BOOK FINANCIALS

The updates always included a report from our finance department. How well did we do during the past month? Did we make money? Did we lose money? Jennifer Anderson, our CFO, created a fun presentation using a big flat-screen that was mounted over the buffet bar. She revealed all the key financial figures to the group: gross revenue, net profit, and all the crucial numbers in between.

If it sounds weird to you that a company would publish their financials for all the employees to see, you're right. It is unusual, but being open and transparent about how and when the company made a profit was crucial to everyone understanding their contribution to the bottom line. How could financial knowledge affect the bottom line? It helped employees make better decisions, and this is key: When people understand how their actions (or inactions) positively (or negatively) affect profitability—and they have a vested interest in that profitability—they pay more attention. They care more. Our employees' vested interest was in our unique profit sharing model that I shared in chapter 6, "A Piece of the Pie."

If we had an especially good month and the profit share was up from the previous period, we celebrated our hard work together. When we had

disappointing results to share—a month in which the profits were lower—
we discussed the factors that contributed to less-than-stellar results. Did
we have equipment failure that necessitated overtime to meet production
needs, thereby adding labor costs? Did we add several new customers
who created a top line surge along with significant on-boarding expense?
Whatever it was that happened, we discussed it so everyone understood the
implications of the contributing factors.

For most employees, this level of transparency was enough. Some
wanted much greater detail. They wanted to know exactly what made up
our cost of goods sold (COGS) down to the penny for every envelope
and every sheet of paper. Did we share that information? Of course we
did! Sometimes that meant sharing the vendor invoices, and sometimes it
meant an even deeper dive.

> " ... it showed that we were listening, that we cared, and that we wanted them to have what they needed to do a great job."

For example, those with inquiring
minds often sat side by side with me or
the CFO. We allowed them to access our
accounting system and peer as deeply as
they cared to into every line item on the
profit and loss (P&L) and balance sheets.
(The only information we did not allow
them to access was individual compensa-
tion figures, which was private.) Our open-book policy was especially help-
ful to the sales team because it gave them the basis for the pricing. And it's
why the sales team was allowed to do their own pricing. We trusted they'd
make good decisions because they had all the necessary data.

We shared information about our company operations and decisions in
numerous ways, but likely the most impactful was publishing the minutes
from our weekly leadership meeting. That meeting was held in the conference room adjacent to our lobby. Employees coming in and out of the
building saw us in there and naturally wondered what we were talking
about. After the meeting, they politely asked about what we discussed.

Did we talk about the frequent paper jams they experienced with the new paper? Or how we needed a new inserter to keep up with the ever-growing volume? Or the new customer whose custom envelope was wreaking havoc and slowing throughput to a crawl?

We understood their curiosity and the need to know that we heard their concerns and that we were addressing the issues that directly impacted them on a daily basis. For full transparency, we published the minutes of our leadership meetings on a large screen in the production area where anyone—including visiting customers or vendors—could read them.

This level of transparency fostered trust and confidence in the leadership team that we could not have achieved otherwise. The information we shared helped everyone make better decisions. And just as important, it showed that we were listening, that we cared, and that we wanted them to have what they needed to do a great job.

A CELEBRATION OF OUR VALUES

The most highly anticipated part of our monthly company meeting was our "Family Member of the Month" ritual. A few days prior to the meeting, the employees received a ballot that listed everyone's name. Thoughtfully, each person selected someone they believed best demonstrated and lived the company values that month. After placing a check by the name, they wrote a few sentences explaining *why* they chose that individual.

After each department presented their reports at the monthly meeting, the votes and accolades for the "Family Member of the Month" were projected onto the flat screen. We had a roving microphone that allowed each employee to read a vote before passing the mic to the next person. Though a few of the votes were silly and fun, all were heartfelt recognition of a coworker who'd gone above and beyond.

The person who received the most votes won the honor of Family Member of the Month and was handed a $100 bill. The person who received the most votes cumulatively throughout the year, demonstrating that they *constantly and consistently* upheld the company values, became Family Member of the Year. Their prize was an all-expense-paid trip to the destination of their choice plus $1,000 cash for spending money. Our theory was that a trip is something that goes beyond the day to day; it's an opportunity to make memories that stick with you forever.

The first person to win the annual honor was Matt Motsinger. He and his wife, Lauren, chose Atlantis in the Bahamas as their destination. Matt sent us several photos from Atlantis but my favorite was a selfie . . . just Matt lounging on a floral chaise, sporting a big grin, holding a cigar and surrounded by $100 bills!

Since most winners chose beach locales, we were all a little surprised when Darius Norman told us he was going to Disney World the year he won the honor. *What?* Disney World? He could go anywhere in the world, and he chose Orlando, Florida? We thought, *Don't you want to lie on a beach somewhere and drink margaritas for heaven's sake? Or ski at Whistler?* Nah, Darius chose Disney, and here's why.

Darius' girlfriend, Dee, had a little boy, Christian, who had never been to Disney, and Darius wanted to take him. It's easy to see why he won this award that was based on a year's worth of living our values. Darius definitely lived the values, and he ultimately got the girl too. Shortly after the trip, Dee and Darius were married, and now Christian has a little brother and a little sister.

There's an expression in the South about people who complain all the time even when there's nothing to complain about. We say that person would "still bitch eating ice cream." From time to time, we had a few of those at LetterLogic. After one company meeting, one of these individuals grumbled to me that Family Member of the Month was nothing more than a popularity contest. I reflected on that complaint a lot. It bothered me, so I asked a few respected coworkers to discuss and debate the issue with me. Should we discontinue the voting system? Was it unfair? Was it rigged?

The defining answer ultimately came from Darius, then in his late twenties. He said "Sherry, you and I have gotten recognition all our lives. We get lots of attention, whether it's deserved or not. But there are so many people in that room who've never gotten positive recognition ever, for anything. You only have to look around the room and see the pride and joy they receive when they hear a coworker brag on them. It's what we are all about. Don't take this away from them!" (Once again, you can see how Darius lived the values.)

Darius was so right. From where I stood at the front of the room during the company meeting, I was able to see the looks on the faces of the individuals who received the vote and compliments as they were read. Without exception, every single person was touched by it. When the votes were greeted by raucous cheers and applause, even the shyest recipients smiled and were able to bask in the glow of acceptance, appreciation, and praise.

There *was* a popularity component to the monthly vote. Because employees who embrace change, take responsibility, care about others, and make work fun DO BECOME POPULAR! That said, when I reviewed the list of Family Member of the Year winners over the years, there was just one employee who had likely been outgoing and popular his whole life. The others were quiet and somewhat introverted. They were all chosen for their consistent practice of living the values day in, day out; for the way they cared for others; *for their empathy.*

THE STATUS QUO SUX

All new employees were required to participate in a few hours of LetterLogic 101. This session, separate from the other on-boarding activities, was an informal opportunity for me to interact directly with each new family member and share the importance of LetterLogic's history and culture. Our time together usually began with a Lunch with Lucy. The 101 session always included a trip to our lobby, where "SQS" was affixed in large letters over the doorway to the production facility. SQS? Yes. It stands for the "Status Quo Sux," which was our company motto.

The motto was born from an illuminating conversation I had with a member of our leadership team over coffee one day. He observed, "Sherry, I've come to realize that no matter how good we are, you're never going to be satisfied, that you'll always push us to be even better." Ouch! I took his words to heart. As I turned his observation inward, reflecting on my own "not good enough" complex, I was filled with shame. I took it to mean that I was not showing proper appreciation, that I was communicating dissatisfaction with the team's efforts.

"Oh no!" I exclaimed. "I am so sorry! I hate that I would make anyone feel that way—that's the opposite of how I feel." He tried to quell my anguish.

"No, Sherry, it's why we're so good! It's why we have the reputation we do, and it's why people want to work here. Because you don't allow us to get complacent. It's a good thing."

Still, I wasn't convinced. I spent all day and a sleepless night worrying that I hadn't demonstrated the proper appreciation for our extraordinary team. I was reading the Jim Collins book *Good to Great* at the time and tried to justify my stance. Who would be happy with just "good"? I *was* always pushing to be "great" and then "greater."

By morning, I'd come to grips with it. My colleague was right. No matter how good we thought we were—no matter how many awards we won, and no matter how fast we grew—I wanted us to constantly strive to be better. To be true to myself, to be authentic, instead of trying to change the perception of my expectations, I decided to be even more direct and vocal about it.

I shared the entire exchange at our next monthly company meeting and announced our new motto: "The Status Quo Sux." Taking it a step further, I told the group, and then told each new employee during their personal LetterLogic 101, that they would never be criticized for trying something new, even if it ended in failure.

Serendipitously, that week I met Ben Skoog, who was an executive at

Louisiana Pacific, a global leader in engineered wood products based in Nashville. He shared one of his key leadership tools with me: a mistake quota. Yes, he encouraged his team members to share their mistakes, so everyone could learn from them.

After speaking with Ben, I initiated our own Mistake Quota Forum. It required that our leaders share the biggest mistake they made in the previous period—personal or professional—at our quarterly planning meeting. The expectation was that they would share their mistake and what they learned from it so we (theoretically) would not make the same mistake.

The Mistake Quota was an amazing way to encourage vulnerability and transparency, encouraging individuals to be their authentic selves and to be open about their mistakes and failures. I opened the session by sharing my own mistakes first, in the hopes that others' mistakes wouldn't seem so awful in comparison. This exercise built trust. My leadership team knew I wasn't going to cover up my own errors, and they didn't need to cover theirs either. It allowed us to build a tighter, more cohesive team that wasn't afraid to try something new to make us better. Thanks, Ben Skoog!

TAKEAWAY BOX:
Transparency and authenticity build trust and reinforce values, which in turn removes the barriers to good communication.

Fourth Course

THE SIDES

11

Bennies à la Carte
Profit Sharing and
Living Wages Aren't Enough

"Notice the small things. The rewards are inversely proportional."

–Liz Vassey

INGREDIENTS:

ATTENTIVENESS AND PURE EMPATHY.

There's no doubt that the heart of the LetterLogic benefits package was our profit sharing program. The whole concept of equal distribution—still one of my best ideas—was intended to show employees they were cared for, valued, and had an equally vital role in the success of the company. But combining the profit share with fair living wages wasn't enough.

We had to have other benefits too; stuff that addressed the real day-to-day needs of our work family and made a real impact on their lives. We didn't have Ping-Pong tables or free beer or unlimited vacation time or any of those other cool perks you've read about. But we did offer tuition reimbursement and paid leave for new moms *and* dads. One by one, we added other benefits that really mattered.

HEALTH INSURANCE

During my first few years in Nashville, I didn't have health insurance. One day, when my daughter Whitney was about five years old, she cut her foot at our apartment complex playground. I cleaned the wound as best I could, and it looked fine for a day or so. But it started looking bad and got steadily worse over the next few days. Without health insurance, or extra money, or even a credit card, I kept hoping for an improvement that didn't come.

Finally, I knew I couldn't wait any longer. I took Whitney to the emergency room and was told she had a staph infection. The pediatrician said if I'd waited any longer, she might have lost her leg or her life. That memory haunted me for years. When I started LetterLogic, I vowed never to let such a thing happen to anyone who worked with me. Long before the Affordable Care Act (commonly known as Obamacare), LetterLogic committed to pay 100 percent of the healthcare, medical, dental, and disability insurance for all employees *and their families*. That was no small feat, and I faced opposition and obstacles along the way.

In the beginning, when there were only three of us, it just seemed like the cost of being in business. It never felt like a burden or something we couldn't afford to do. The thought of offering less than 100 percent coverage never entered my mind, because the memory of not having insurance was still vivid.

After our third or fourth year in business, an employee questioned the fairness of the company policy. I didn't understand how anyone could question the fairness of a free health insurance program. However, he told me his health coverage—as a single young man—had to be much less expensive than the coverage for married employees with children. He thought it unfair that we spent more money on insurance for employees with families. He insisted that the fair and equitable thing to do was to pay him the difference as a monthly bonus. I was shocked. Stunned.

Yes, of course I was aware of the difference, but it had never occurred to me that an employee would think it unfair. The idea was ludicrous. Nevertheless, I consulted an attorney who determined there might be some liability. It was the first time in business I was faced with the reality that "fair" and "equal" are not the same thing. The lawyer advised us to cover only the employees and have them pay for family policies or policy upgrades individually.

> "It was the first time in business I was faced with the reality that 'fair' and 'equal' are not the same thing."

I will never forget the company meeting when I announced we were discontinuing the paid family coverage. From that point on, LetterLogic would pay for employee coverage only, and each employee was responsible for his or her own family coverage. I cried then, and I cry now telling you about it.

Throughout the years, insurance coverage and options have become more and more complex. Some employees wanted higher deductibles and others wanted no co-pay or other options. It became necessary to provide a menu of options to choose from, and the company offered an insurance "allowance" for employees to spend as they chose.

The funny thing about insurance coverage is that every potential hire clamors for insurance coverage, and every employee gladly uses it. However, they seldom consider the enormous expense of a perk, or a benefit, that is gifted to them. After a short time, they take it for granted. That realization led me to mandate a biannual report for each employee to show them how much money the company spent on their behalf. It provided context for our monthly financial reports, where employees saw a huge dollar amount on the line item attributed to "Insurance."

HOME-BUYING ASSISTANCE

Do you remember the first time you bought a house? Do you remember how exciting and scary it was? I do. I remember every detail, although it was over thirty years ago. The house was a long-neglected brick Tudor on the fringes of a questionable neighborhood. It had three bedrooms but not even one fully functioning bath. The ceramic tile in the shower was long gone, but the previous owners had used the shower anyway, rotting the plaster walls right down to the studs and the joists beneath.

I took out a mortgage to buy the house and a small bridge loan to renovate the bathroom. One of the proudest moments of my life was when I moved into that house (owned by First American Bank and me). I had moved to Nashville with no money and worked hard to save enough to qualify for a mortgage. Buying a home was a rite of passage into adulthood, an experience that validated and satisfied me in ways I couldn't have imagined.

Years later, when LetterLogic was growing steadily, I often talked to employees about home ownership and how it could be the foundation for building personal wealth. Remembering the pride I'd felt, I encouraged them to save money to buy their first homes. I decided the company could participate in the initiative and help with a cash gift toward the down payment or closing costs. Thus began our First-Time Home-Buyers Gift.

In the early years, our gifts ranged from $1,000 to $10,000, depending on the employee's individual needs. We were careful to make sure we counseled them not to get in over their heads, not to buy a house they couldn't really afford. In all, we helped at least nineteen individuals buy their first homes. Helping young people shift their focus from buying brand new cars to saving money for a home, an asset that would gain value, was very gratifying.

Coincidentally, one of my most soul-satisfying home-ownership experiences happened *after* the sale of LetterLogic in 2016. Soon after I announced that the company had been sold, I met with each employee, and based on their company tenure, gave them a cash gift. For a few hours, I understood how it must feel to be Oprah ("You get a car. You get a car. You get a car!"). It was so much fun to hand my coworkers checks and ask what they planned to do with the money.

"I'm going to pay off my student loans."

"On the way home, I'm buying that fishing boat I've wanted all my life."

"A new roof! This couldn't come at a better time."

It was an unforgettable way to say goodbye to the women and men who'd helped me build our remarkable company. But the best was yet to come. Two

> "Gorica said it was the company culture that inspired her to look beyond her own needs and wants."

months after the company was sold and the gifts were distributed, one of the production employees, Gorica Zivak, invited me to lunch. She wanted to give me an update on how she'd spent her gift.

Gorica saved all the money from the profit sharing program and combined it with her gift money to pay off the mortgage on her parents' home. This twenty-five-year-old woman had paid off her mom and dad's mortgage! Unbelievable. What an amazing young woman. Gorica said it was the company culture that inspired her to look beyond her own needs and wants. It was one of the proudest moments of my career.

BRING YOUR KIDS TO WORK

When I first moved to Nashville, I didn't have any friends or relatives to help me with childcare, and affordable daycare was not readily available. Even when I finally found a decent one, there were other challenges to overcome. Most childcare facilities are closed on holidays, and there were some holidays that my employers didn't observe. I was expected to be at work, but there was no one to care for my child.

Then there were the "snow days. " In Nashville, the mere potential of snow signals everyone to drop whatever they're doing and run like crazy to the grocery store. In a matter of a few hours, every gallon of milk and loaf of bread is gone from the shelves, and the whole city hunkers down to wait for the snow, which usually never comes. Those days are hell for single parents. And, of course, there are always the inevitable colds and viruses that run through daycare facilities like wildfire during the winter months. As soon as a child has a runny nose, a cough, or a slight fever, they aren't allowed in daycare.

These real-life situations sound like minor inconveniences unless you're the parent who has to figure out what to do. Then you know exactly how frustrating this is. The daycare centers close, but work doesn't. What the heck are you going to do with your kid? You won't get paid if you don't get to work. There's no one to take care of your child, so you must stay home, losing a day's wages and wreaking havoc on an already strained household budget.

The employer loses out too, because your work either goes undone and piles up or is loaded onto someone else, which may cause the company to incur overtime expenses. This problem was especially challenging for my small company. We were lean staffed to begin with, and we raced against the clock every day. No matter how many folks we had on the production floor, and no matter how large the production volume was, we promised our customers that their mail would be processed and delivered to the post office within twenty-four hours of receiving their data. A missing employee or two could totally derail us.

With the not-too-distant memories of my single-parent struggles, the next benefit move at LetterLogic seemed like a logical no-brainer. We instituted a policy that allowed all employees to bring their kids to work whenever they needed to. They didn't have to spend even a minute worrying about what to do. They just loaded up the kids and brought them to work. Though we welcomed kids at LetterLogic, we didn't have an official in-house daycare area, so the child or children stayed with their parents in their office or cubicle. We made other arrangements for people who worked in the production area, since it was unsafe to have children in that area. "Other" arrangements sometimes meant I was the babysitter.

I vividly recall the snowy day when my office was filled with children all afternoon. School had been let out early in anticipation of snow, so I offered to entertain the kids while their parents got the mail out. We raided the snack machine a few times, made popcorn, battered each other with Nerf-balls and spitballs, and went wild with scissors and construction paper until almost 7:00 p.m. when the workday was over. I was worn out and left the huge mess in my office to clean up the following morning.

When I returned to work the next day, Harvey, our custodian, greeted me in the lobby to warn me that someone had trashed my office. He was taken aback when I started laughing, and then he was relieved when I told him I'd hosted a party with a mob of kids and would clean up the mess myself.

Now, you can argue that having the CEO of a multimillion-dollar company babysitting for the employees' kids was not the "highest and best use" of my time—nor was it "majoring in the majors." But on those rare occasions when I was able to contribute to our "family" in this way, it was fun and rewarding.

On snow days and during official school holidays, it was a joy to have children at work with us. Yes, it was a distraction sometimes, but I wanted our employees to feel confident that it was okay. They could still earn a full day's pay without added childcare expenses. The simple elegance of this solution inspired loyalty and supported the family atmosphere for which we were known.

You might guess that it was mostly moms who brought children to work, but dads brought theirs too. The first time one of our dads utilized the policy, his child was only two weeks old, and his wife had a full day of doctor's appointments. The dad came in, somewhat timidly, with a tiny infant in his little carrier. He didn't quite know what to do, but his coworkers took over! They fought over that baby all day. Everyone took turns feeding him, changing diapers, and fawning over this beautiful baby boy while his proud papa watched and worked and beamed.

> "Having our coworkers' 'real' families around the office led us all to be more compassionate and understanding of each other's circumstances."

There's an interesting side benefit to having kids at work. It allows you to see your coworkers in a whole new light. Meeting their kids and seeing how they interact together offers a different filter and a richer depth to what makes them tick. Having our coworkers' "real" families around the office led us all to be more compassionate and understanding of each other's circumstances. It also fostered a renewed respect for them as parents.

PERSONAL LOANS

Employees who found themselves in a financial pinch had the option to borrow money from the company. The goal was to protect our team members from borrowing from predatory payday lenders and their exorbitant fees. Loan repayment was set up with paycheck deductions that fit the individual circumstance. We did have some guidelines in place, but there were no strings attached to the money, and the "application process" was simple. For the first several years, if someone needed a loan, they came to me, and I approved or declined the request on the spot.

The loan program evolved and improved when we hired Jennifer Anderson as our controller. If you look up the word "integrity" in the dictionary, you'll see her photo. She is the epitome of honor, honesty, earnestness, and financial responsibility. Jennifer challenged me to think differently about the loan program. From where she sat, the loan program wasn't about whether we could afford to help the person or not, but whether we were truly helping them or enabling them to continue to manage their money poorly. She saw it as an opportunity to teach people about money management, potentially a more valuable gift than providing cash loans. She insisted that we could continue to be compassionate and generous but that the loan program needed to include lessons in money management skills. Teaching these skills is actually more loving and empathetic in the long run than lending people the money.

I got to test Jennifer's theory when the next employee asked for a loan. He wanted to buy a car, a large luxury SUV. Because he had a poor credit rating, he couldn't qualify for the loan without a sizable down payment. With Jennifer's challenge fresh in my mind, instead of my usual knee-jerk reaction of just writing a check, I sat with him and asked a few questions. The point was to get him to think about the financial implications of his proposed purchase and loan.

Our conversation went something like this:

- That's a beautiful car. I'll bet the insurance is going to be expensive. Heck, let's call the insurance company right now and see what the coverage will be. WOW! $290 a month! That's a lot, isn't it?

- What is the gas mileage for this car? What? It's only 10 mpg in city driving? Since you'll be driving it to and from work each day, ten miles each way, plus chauffeuring the kids on the weekends, looks like you'll be spending at least $100 a week on gas. That's a lot, isn't it?

- Oops, I almost forgot. What about the monthly payment? If we loan you $10,000 for the down payment, and you pay the company back at the rate of $100 per paycheck, you will be taking home $100 less each week and then you have a huge car note too. What? The note is going to be $600 a month? That's an awful lot, isn't it?

- I know you're hoping to buy a house in the next few years. Have you considered how the purchase of this vehicle might affect that dream? Think about it. With interest rates so low right now, you can own a home for less than the monthly expense of owning this car. Instead of a fancy car, you could buy a house. That's amazing, isn't it?

Even after raising these points, the employee still wanted to move forward with the loan, but I had to decline. It wasn't that I wanted to dictate how he managed his money. I just couldn't, in good conscience, enable him to go more deeply in debt to purchase a depreciating asset.

And thus began the practice of having potential borrowers meet with Jennifer, instead of me, to vet their need for a loan. Once she started tracking the loans, it became obvious there were a handful of individuals who were constantly borrowing. As soon as they paid off one loan, they were back asking for another, sometimes in just a matter of days. Jennifer suggested we limit the number of loans a person could have in a calendar year. She met with our habitual borrowers for financial coaching and training on how to work out a personal budget. In this way, she was extremely influential in the financial health of many of our employees. Though she is a young woman herself, she helped others to "grow up" and become financially responsible. The result of Jennifer's compassionate stewardship was that we were much more thoughtful in lending. She ensured we were actually helping our employees instead of perpetuating a problem.

This was certainly the case with an employee who bought his first home with a little help from us. Though he had a good credit score and easily qualified for a mortgage, he had a very expensive car and immediately felt the impact of the car note, insurance, his mortgage, and other expenses. Wisely, he worked out a plan to sell the car and decided to walk or take the bus the two miles to work every day until his finances were more manageable. For eighteen months, rain or shine, snow or sleet, he walked or took the bus to work, until he was able to pay cash for a car—a car that was even nicer than the first one.

ENTREPRENEURSHIP ASSISTANCE

At most companies, if you're operating a small business on the side or moonlighting to build your own enterprise, you'd best keep your boss from finding out. Not at LetterLogic.

We encouraged employees to be open with us if they wanted to own their own businesses and offered advice, mentoring, and financial assistance. Since the entrepreneurship path had been so good to me, I wanted to afford others the opportunity, too. I wish more employees had taken advantage of this perk, but the handful who did are doing well with their own enterprises.

One of our beneficiaries started a graphic design and sign-making company, Pro Graphic South, during his early days at LetterLogic. When he needed funds to upgrade his sign-printing equipment, we were excited to help, although he could have easily gotten a business loan. Ironically, the program was designed to help employees with *their* businesses, but with Patrick, there was a reverse mentoring relationship. I regularly sought advice and guidance from Patrick instead of the other way around. His business instincts and insight were invaluable to me through the years. To this day, Pro Graphic South is a flourishing business.

THE THREE BEARS

At one point, LetterLogic owned three vehicles named after the Three Bears story: Papa Bear, Mama Bear, and Baby Bear.

Mama Bear was a mid-size box truck used to transport the pallets of mail to the post office each day. Baby Bear was a small Nissan pickup truck, dented and ugly, but still a bargain when we bought her for $1,200. We used her for running errands or picking up supplies. Papa Bear was a much larger box truck we used when our mail volume became too much for Mama Bear alone to hold.

I found myself borrowing Baby Bear and Mama Bear for personal use every now and then if I needed to move furniture or haul a bunch of plants.

I decided to offer the company trucks to employees to use as needed on weekends too. I wanted to give them the convenience of access to a few large vehicles and save them from having to rent one. The only stipulation was that the trucks be refueled and cleaned for the next business day.

Most of the employees used a "bear" at least once. They used them for hauling mulch, for moving to a new house or apartment, for a Saturday morning of yard sales, and a hundred other things. It wasn't as official as the other benefits, but it certainly was a great perk we all took advantage of.

Eventually our mail volume grew to the point that we qualified to have the USPS drop a trailer at our dock each morning and return to haul it away each day at 7:00 p.m. We no longer needed Mama Bear and Papa Bear. We sold Papa Bear and gifted Mama Bear to Safe Haven, a shelter for homeless families. We eventually gifted Baby Bear to Paul, our very own "MacGyver"—the only employee likely to keep her running for another thirty years with just some duct tape and a paper clip.

WE ALSO SPILLED SOME MILK

I've talked a lot about the great benefits offered at LetterLogic, but there were also a few that didn't work out so well. I want to tell you about those too, in the hope that I can prevent you from making the same mistakes or to encourage you to find a better way to do what we were trying to do.

Gym memberships and on-site gyms: For years, we paid for YMCA gym memberships for employees to influence healthy living. But we had tons of space in our building, and I thought, *Why not have a gym right here at work?* We invited all the employees to donate any abandoned workout equipment they had at home. Before too long, we had a plethora of machines and gadgets including a treadmill, free weights, and a rowing machine. The company pitched in and created a decent little work-out area in one corner of the factory. A handful of us used it.

A few years later, we hired a new employee who happened to be a fitness maniac. He was enthralled with the CrossFit craze and asked if we could build a gym. I proudly told him we already had a gym and walked him over to see it. Shaking his head, he was adamant that what we had was a geriatric playground. He began a relentless quest for a "real gym."

Before long, he convinced me to give him space in an abandoned dock bay, along with a decent budget to build a gym. While we were completing the gym, we discovered that another employee was a certified CrossFit trainer, and before we knew it, the budget was exceeded by 100 percent. Nevertheless, in a matter of a few weeks, we had a very respectable gym and two individuals who were passionate about CrossFit. They eagerly set up fitness routines for everyone who was interested.

At first, the response and results were amazing. One employee lost forty pounds in the first two months. It was great to go to work out and find a handful of employees in the gym encouraging each other. But you can probably guess what happened. The novelty wore off. Everyone got "too busy" or it was too hot or too cold in the gym. Before long, just one or two employees used the gym.

It's funny now, but when we were building the gym, I was bragging about it to a local entrepreneur. He chuckled and told me it was a waste of money. I remember thinking that he might have had a bad experience with a similar venture, but *we* were different. We weren't. The truth is that if someone wants to make the gym a part of their lifestyle, they will, and they'll be willing to pony up the money for the membership. I don't regret adding the gym (either of them) because I learned a valuable lesson, but I wouldn't offer them again.

Healthy snacks: I would frame this perk in the "trying to influence behavior" category, but it might belong in the "can't please everyone" category. Or perhaps both. Our receptionist started putting a bowl of mini candy bars on the front desk—those "bite size" chocolates and caramels that make you want to go back for more. The reception desk became a popular gathering spot, and before long, he was refilling a large bowl several times a day.

I resisted for a while, but around 3:30 or 4:00 p.m., it sure was tempting to go grab a little sugar boost.

Soon enough, a few people started to complain about the lack of healthy snack choices. (They were members of the "people who will bitch while eating ice cream" crowd.) As is my nature, I wanted to make everyone happy, and that resulted in two changes. First, the chocolates were replaced with a bowl of fruit. Second, the vending machine was emptied of its sugar and salt-filled processed snack foods and restocked with purportedly healthier snacks. The silver lining was that it rarely had to be restocked because hardly anyone ate that stuff! In the end, I decided we paid everyone well enough that they could provide their own snacks. Call me Scrooge.

Smoking cessation: I went through a phase where I went from aggravated to livid when I saw the smokers (several times a day!) leave their work areas and go to the back dock to smoke. It drove me crazy to see how their coworkers had to pick up the slack. In the smoker's mind, it was "just a five-minute smoke break" but the reality is that most of the time, the breaks lasted closer to twenty-five minutes. No one ever just stayed five minutes because there were other smokers out there, and everyone got involved in a conversation. Before long, they were on their second cigarette and fifteen minutes had gone by. Then they needed a bathroom break, and when you added it up, they've missed twenty-five minutes of work.

Thinking I could solve any problem with a policy, I started a new one that stipulated you must clock out for a smoke break (I still like that one), and you could not smoke on company property. People who wanted to smoke had to either walk down the street away from the office or drive off the property.

Unfortunately, requiring employees to clock out for smoke breaks wasn't a policy that could be fairly enforced. A few salaried employees smoked, and as such, they didn't clock in and out and were therefore not "docked" like the hourly employees. Once again, I was face-to-face with the inequities in the business world.

To add a carrot along with the stick (though it was hard to decide which was which), we paid for a smoking cessation program. No matter what method anyone wanted to use to stop, the company would pay for it. Over the years, we paid for Nicorette patches and gum and even hypnotherapy.

The good news was that many employees quit smoking. The bad news is that most of them started again. I learned that behavior couldn't be mandated and expected to stick. I also finally realized that I couldn't push my own ideas and health values onto others. Eventually, people go home, and what they did at home was none of my business.

THE BIGGEST LESSON

What's the biggest lesson I learned with all the benefits—those that lasted and those that didn't? I learned to stop reacting to all the trendy benefits I read about, and I got to know my employees better so I understood what mattered to *them*. I carefully considered which programs would enhance the company culture, contributing to an environment where employees could grow, flourish, and feel appreciated. In so doing, *the company* saw measurable positive results:

- Happy, well-cared-for employees are more loyal to the company. They are not tempted away by every offer that comes their way. Even by the most conservative estimates around the cost of turnover, keeping good people saves thousands of dollars *per employee*.

- Loyal, focused employees produce better products and services that customers are willing to pay more for. This has a real, tangible effect on the bottom line.

- Happy customers will remain loyal when your competitors come after them. They won't leave you when they are offered a cheaper alternative.

Investing in your employees is just smart business. You might ask, "But what happens if you invest in them and they leave you?" I ask you, "What happens if you don't and they stay?"

TAKEAWAY BOX:

Consider the demographics and psychographics of your team and provide benefits that matter to THEM.

12

Booth or Table?
Organizational Charts and Titles

"Sitting at the table doesn't make you a diner, unless you eat some of what's on that plate."

–Malcolm X

INGREDIENTS:

CLARITY.

For the first few years at LetterLogic, we didn't need an organization chart. There were just a handful of us, and we all knew our roles; we reported to each other. Having a flat organizational structure suited me just fine and seemed to fit our culture too. But as we grew and individual roles became departments, those departments naturally needed a leader. Things had to change.

Our first official org chart was drafted for the sole purpose of showing each person where they fit, where they needed to go for guidance, and where to turn to escalate a matter if they weren't getting what they needed from their supervisors. At that time, we didn't have a dedicated human resources director. Our office manager created a traditional functional org chart for me based on titles. The resulting document floored me, and not in a good way.

When we were all assigned to spots on the chart, I, as the CEO, sat at the top, but Patrick Johnson, one of the most valuable contributors (and one of the finest individuals I've ever known), was at the bottom. It bothered me so badly that I didn't sleep that night. Let me tell you about Patrick, and you'll understand why.

In 2003, LetterLogic started getting some press. *The Nashville Business Journal* wrote about the company and our efforts to put the employees' needs first. A few days after the article ran, Patrick Johnson walked into our lobby for the first time. He'd read about our culture in the *Journal* and wanted to work with us.

Patrick is a quiet, reserved, handsome man who exudes physical strength and athleticism. In fact, my first impression was that he could be a body double for Steve McNair (the then-quarterback for the Tennessee Titans). He had a depth of experience in the printing/fulfillment industry, but we didn't have any job openings at the time. Unbelievably, he was willing to work for LetterLogic without pay just to be able to help an organization that was trying to live its values and respect its people. He was sincere, but I couldn't very well promote a "valuing our people" narrative and let someone work without pay. I told him I'd call when a position became available and we could afford him. That occasion came a few months later, and it was my pleasure to hire him.

Patrick proved to be an ideal coworker and team member. Even now, years later, I have a hard time describing him as an "employee." His primary job was to operate the high-speed laser printers that produced the physical documents we mailed each day. But he eventually served as my mentor, the voice of reason, and our moral compass. And he was unstoppable. I don't know how he did it, but no matter how much we grew, no matter how much volume we added, he handled it. There was no drama and no fanfare; the work just got done. But that's not all. With dignity and kindness and without ego, he quietly coached those around him. He led by example and proved to be the rock that we all leaned on in hard times.

As our workload continued to grow, and we had to expand to two shifts, Patrick volunteered to move to the night shift. That meant he worked

> " ... we were all equally valuable and equally essential to producing a great service and product."

alone in a 27,000-square-foot factory. Alone. Every night, by himself, he set the company up for success the next day. When the rest of us got to work in the morning, Patrick had already completed much of the printing needed for the day, so we could then move the work through the additional steps and processes on time. Do you remember the fairytale about the shoemaker and the elves? The shoemaker would leave his shop at night, and when he came into work the following morning, elves had turned heaps of raw leather into the finest shoes, which the shoemaker was able to sell immediately, buying even more leather to leave behind. We were the shoemaker, leaving more and more work behind for Patrick each evening, and he then turned that raw data into hundreds of thousands of statements and invoices. He didn't complain. He didn't ask for more money. He didn't ask for an assistant.

And there I was, looking at an org chart that put me at the top and Patrick, my mentor and invaluable team member, at the bottom. It wasn't just words and boxes on a sheet of paper anymore. The visual story was a violation of everything I knew to be true—we were all equally valuable and equally essential to producing a great service and product.

SPOKES ON A WHEEL: EVERYONE IS ESSENTIAL

I struggled to create a diagram that would illustrate our various roles in a way that didn't imply that some of those positions were less important. How could a chart with lines and boxes ever communicate how much faith we had in Patrick and how much we relied on him? How could a traditional org chart show that our inimitable receptionist, the one and only Frank P. LaVarre, was not just the person who answered the phone and opened the door, but our Mr. Congeniality, our resident scientist and astronomist, our linguist and grammar-checker, our poet, and most of all, our friend who would do anything for us, and anything for anyone?

Using the image of a bicycle wheel, with the CEO at the hub and the spokes representing the various departments, we designed a chart that more effectively communicated how interdependent we all were. Building on the idea, we used gears to portray our organizational structure; gears of various sizes that each performed a vital function and synchronized work with others. If one gear did not function properly, the entire machine stopped. Maybe we could limp along for a while, but we would not operate as smoothly. Everyone was essential to making our world turn.

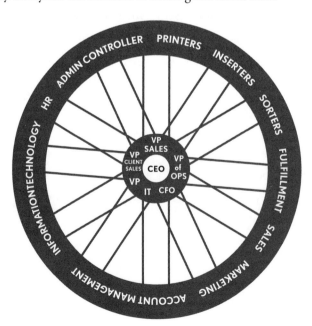

As we got bigger, eventually we devolved into using the traditional org-chart setup again, and I regretted that I allowed that to happen. As we gained more notoriety, and our hires were more polished and sophisticated, I felt I needed to adapt, and I made our foundational documents less creative. Now, in hindsight, I can see how our own authentic way of eliminating hierarchical layers was actually more modern, more progressive, and perfect for us and for the time.

DISHING OUT JOB TITLES

Like many entrepreneurs, when I started LetterLogic, I handed out titles like candy. After all, I named myself—the person with no formal education and no leadership experience—chief executive officer. Appointing someone vice president seemed an innocuous way to incentivize and reward. However, it turns out, giving someone a title they haven't earned, and for which they aren't prepared, can do harm to the individual and create needless drama for the company.

By the time I learned the dangers of over-titling, I'd made the mistake too many times (as you will see in the examples here), each time facing difficult conversations. Basically, I had to do one of three things:

- Take the title away (with as much kindness and compassion as possible) and hope the person had the humility to accept the move and continue working for the company.
- Terminate employment.
- Allow the person to continue with the title while pushing and pulling them along, hoping they'd grow into the role.

An employee I'll call Sylvia was an aggressive, hardworking woman who originally came to work at LetterLogic as a printer operator. She had an outgoing personality and became the go-to person in production. In her first performance review, I gave her a substantial raise and named her vice president of operations. It seemed like an appropriate move at the time. But it wasn't.

In those early years, the company was growing by 100 percent or more per year. When we were generating $8,000 a day in revenue, I was just trying to keep us on track. I wasn't looking ahead to a time when we would produce $16,000 a day, or $50,000 a day, or $100,000 a day—or ultimately, $150,000 a day.

When I gave Sylvia her new title, I overlooked some leadership weaknesses and her limited interest in, or capacity for, learning. I wasn't thinking about what would be needed in a much larger organization. Unfortunately, when the size of the staff and the complexity of the workflow and machinery increased, but Sylvia wasn't growing along with us, I realized she couldn't fulfill the title or the necessary accompanying responsibilities. I was going to have to "untitle" her.

To soften the impact, I didn't decrease her compensation. I foolishly told myself that anyone would be okay with less work for the same pay, even if it meant a lesser title. I was wrong again. Sylvia couldn't get past losing the vice president of operations title, and she resigned. We lost a well-trained industry veteran and a valuable employee. If I had been more thoughtful and intentional when it came to handing out titles, she would likely have been a solid contributor with us for years.

Looking back on this painful experience, I know what I should have done differently. Instead of carelessly attaching a broad executive title to Sylvia, I should have invested in her training and education. I should have paid for her to take off-site courses in leadership and technology. Investing in her in that way would have been rewarding for her. She *and* the company would have benefitted from her new skills and knowledge. Instead, we lost a hardworking and valuable employee.

Sometimes, over-titling leads to a person becoming (aptly named) "entitled." Some people start to believe that the basic rules don't apply to them. Again, I found this out the hard way.

"John" was a brilliant young man, wise beyond his years, when I hired him. I was so impressed with his intelligence that I didn't hesitate to give him multiple promotions within a short period, each with an even more impressive title. Very quickly, he became one of the most powerful people in our organization with the title to prove it.

Unfortunately, I hadn't considered the emotional maturity necessary to judiciously exercise the power that came with the title. I had not created enough layers of oversight or safeguards on his authority. Ultimately, John began to believe his power was limitless and began making decisions and moves that were beneficial only to him. The only choice I had was to part ways with John. I don't blame him. I blame myself for handing him a title and position of authority without first allowing him to demonstrate the maturity, integrity, and humility necessary for the role.

Then, there was the time I over-titled someone who simply didn't have the drive or the grit to get the job done. He had integrity. He was smart. But no matter how much I coached, prodded, or challenged him, he still wouldn't perform to my minimum standards. I liked him so much, though, that I kept hoping and hoping (even though I know hope is not a strategy) that he'd wake up some day and "get it." He didn't. In his case, at least he knew he wasn't pulling his weight, and he resigned.

SEND IT BACK: WHY ENTREPRENEURS OVER-TITLE

Almost every successful entrepreneur I know has a story about over-titling. It's a prevalent practice, and I wanted to understand why. So I asked, "What led you to advance the person to such a powerful position?" "Why did you promote someone even when you knew she did not fully embrace and reflect company values?" "You'd only known him a few months when you made him COO. What led you to believe he could handle the role?"

The responses followed a few common themes, all of which resonated with me.

Imposter Syndrome

The first justification for over-titling tracked to the phenomenon called "imposter syndrome." Until recently, I thought only females experienced imposter syndrome, but male entrepreneurs told me they felt it too. Imposter syndrome occurs when someone experiences a certain measure of success and somehow believes they didn't earn it, or they don't deserve it, or it's just a matter of time until someone exposes them for the fraud they are. This feeling can push entrepreneurs to appoint the wrong person to a key position, especially when that person has an impressive resume or degree.

> "He said it took him years to find the confidence to accept that he was the best leader for his company."

One of these very successful entrepreneurs told me that at one point he hired someone into the role of president because he was convinced he had just stumbled on success and thought he needed someone smarter than himself to maintain the momentum. The funny thing is, this entrepreneur has an MBA. His new president turned out to be a disaster, and within a few months, he was fired. It's one thing to hire individuals who are smarter than you or who have the skills you lack; it's another for those individuals to usurp your leadership and pursue their own agendas.

Do you think this business owner learned his lesson after that bad experience? No, like me, he made the same mistake multiple times. Why would a smart and successful business owner continue to make the same mistake? He said it took him years to find the confidence to accept that he was the best leader for his company. That hard-earned confidence finally allowed him to hire a leadership team that complemented his skill set instead of eclipsing it.

Running from Responsibilities

Other entrepreneurs told me they over-titled because, in hindsight, they were shirking their responsibilities. They were tired and overworked and mistakenly thought that giving someone a weighty title would push the promoted person to take on more work, thereby lightening the load for the entrepreneur. I'm here to tell you, since I've done that too, it absolutely does not work.

Big Titles, Small Returns

Finally, one business owner told me he over-titled because he thought having individuals leading his young company with titles like CTO, COO, and CMO would give his company credibility. He thought a heavy cadre of C-suite executives would make his company appear to be bigger and more successful than they really were. He learned (the hard way) that having the wrong people at the helm weakened the company and damaged its credibility.

All About Titles

If I could go back in time and mentor my younger self, I'd emphasize the following keys points:

1. **A title is not just a title.**
   Have you noticed what happens when someone gets promoted and their title changes? Within minutes, they've updated their email signature and their LinkedIn profile, proudly displaying the new title. Before the day is over, they've ordered new business cards.

continued

A title tells the rest of the world how important the individual is within the organization and how much authority they have. It indicates the relative likelihood the person has of being a decision maker. By giving a certain title, the CEO is stating to the world that this person was chosen to represent the company in this capacity, thereby "endorsing" them and their behavior.

2. **Don't over-title.**

Over-titling an individual can create confusion in the organization—blurring lines about who is responsible for what tasks. Titles, especially broad, ambiguous titles, can be frustrating for the title-bearer as well as their coworkers.

3. **Everyone has their own set of motivators.**

There was a time I offered equity in the form of phantom stock to an employee whose role was becoming more pivotal. I could tell he was happy to get the stock, but still not satisfied, so I just talked with him about what he wanted. A title. He wanted some outward symbol of his value to the company. His vice president title was appropriate because it had been earned.

4. **Don't hire or title the person based on what you need today.**

Look ahead and identify what skills and attributes will be needed down the road in three to five years. Can the person you're considering for a title promotion fill the role when the company is at $5 million or $10 million or $25 million as opposed to $1 million? Does the person have what it takes to navigate a fast growth trajectory?

ORG CHARTS IN AN EMPATHETIC BUSINESS MODEL

So, do you need an org chart or a title structure in an empathetic leadership business model? If you have empathy for one another, everything will just work itself out without one, right? No. It won't. Without organization and specific role assignments, there will be uncertainty and chaos. To quote Calvin Coolidge, the thirtieth president of the United States, "The only difference between a mob and a trained army is organization."

Good organizational charts and proper titling provide comfort and safety in healthy companies. They allow team members to know what person they should go to first for support, and where to turn next if need be. Structure shows them they are part of a team, and it illustrates how that team provides value to the other teams. From the leadership perspective, a good org chart is necessary for growing and scaling the company. It indicates when a team has grown too large and unwieldy for one person to manage.

TAKEAWAY BOX:

It's all about thoughtfulness, intention, and caring. Employees feel appreciated and nurtured when they fully understand where they fit in and when they understand there are no throwaway titles in your company.

13

Push Away from the Table
The Power of Saying "No"

"The difference between successful people and really successful people is that really successful people say no to almost everything."

–Warren Buffett

INGREDIENTS:

STRENGTH AND GRACE.

I think I speak for most entrepreneurs when I say that "no" was not in our vocabulary—at least in the beginning. We say "yes" to way too many things. We get into the habit of thinking that every ask validates us in some way and that responding to every ask will somehow pay off somewhere down the road. When I reflect on my history as a business leader, it's easy for me to identify the times I said yes when I should have said no. I could fill a book with examples. But it's also easy for me to see the crucial times I said no and how much saying no contributed to our success.

For example, if I'd said yes to any of the first five offers to finance my company, I wouldn't be sharing my story with you now. I would never have had the chance to run the company the way I wanted to run it. I'd have been beholden to investors who would not have agreed to an employee-first culture. But my gut and my hardheadedness stepped up and stopped me from saying yes to them. Instead,

> "…if I'd said yes to any of the first five offers to finance my company, I wouldn't be sharing my story with you now."

I bootstrapped the company until I found an investor who didn't insist on majority ownership and who was okay with my unorthodox leadership. That has made all the difference in the world.

I learned the hard way (and I keep learning) that saying no not only opens more doors; it opens better doors. Here are some of the situations where I should have said no, but didn't.

NO TO PARTNERSHIPS

Dave Ramsey, author of *Financial Peace*, said, "the only ships that don't sail are partnerships." I have to agree with his observation. Obviously, some partnerships do work out fine, but I'd hazard a guess that those partnerships have strict operating agreements, good buy-sell agreements, and involve people of uncommonly high integrity.

Many people who know my company and me are not aware that I started LetterLogic with a 50/50 partner, a dear friend. She didn't have the funds to invest in the business, but she knew the industry. On top of that, she was a good salesperson, and she was my best and most trusted friend who'd been with me through thick and thin. What could possibly go wrong?

Just about everything.

Within eleven months, our friendship and partnership imploded. I had said yes to the idea of having a partner, but we neglected to set up clearly established expectations, and as a result, we each grew angry with and disappointed by the other. There was a range of things that started piling up. It was the realization that both of us were flying to Chicago and Boston and Dallas to do sales presentations, but that I had done all the prep work. And I had done all the talking. It would have been cheaper had I just traveled alone. It was returning from a three-day road trip where I'd driven to Memphis, Little Rock, Dallas, Mobile, and then Atlanta and met with prospective clients in every city, only to return exhausted to find her leaving for the day because, after all, it was 5:01 p.m. I had said yes to a 50/50 split in ownership when I simply did not know that, because I was providing the financing and would fulfill the principal leadership role, I should have had the lion's share of the ownership. In my naïveté, I had wanted to believe that we would be equal contributors work-wise, even though I knew in my gut it wouldn't be so.

Before the end of our first year in business, in a moment of exhaustion and frustration, I lashed out verbally at my partner and my friend. I said unkind things and harshly criticized her about how she spent her time versus how I spent mine. Sadly, it was the last conversation I ever had with her.

The next day I received a letter from her attorney requesting that I buy her half of the business. I was furious. I had provided all the funding for our start-up and felt I'd *given* her half of the business by way of our 50/50 ownership split. Now I had to buy it back from her? I was also deeply saddened. Within a few hours, our friendship and partnership were permanently dissolved, and I became 100 percent owner of LetterLogic. It turned out to be the best financial investment of my life, but it came at a very high cost: the loss of a dear friend.

NO TO NEW PRODUCTS/SERVICES

There's not a CEO anywhere more biased toward their sales team than I was toward mine. I believe the sales team is the lifeblood of any company, probably because my own sales career propelled me to where I am today. If the sales team isn't selling, then there's nothing for the rest of us to do. It doesn't matter how good the product or service is. If no one sells it, nothing happens. My passion for the sales team led me to saying yes to them too often. Sales would approach me with something new that a customer or prospect asked for, and stress to me how crucial that new ask was to keeping or winning business. I'd jump on the wagon with them and immediately reallocate resources to accommodate the request. These knee-jerk reactions weren't good for the company.

> "And this is where the value of transparency in our financials was illuminated."

I especially remember the request for a build-out ancillary to one of our core services. The sales team said several customers had asked for it, so we built it. And no one bought it. I mean, even the customers who said they wanted it didn't buy it, so we made no money on it.

Eventually, after more than one of these scenarios, my advisor Brad Stevens and CFO Jennifer Anderson prodded me to start saying no to the sales team—sort of. Instead of just instantly saying yes, I began asking questions such as:

- If we build this, how many customers are going to buy it?

- How do you propose we pay for it?

- Will the customer be willing to pay for the development of this product they claim to so desperately need?

- How long will they commit to using it?

- Are you so sure you need this to keep or close new business that you are willing to forego commission on this particular piece until the development costs are recouped?

- If we change the focus of our IT and financial resources to this product, which of the current projects do you want us to postpone?

In other words, we placed some of the ROI burden of proof for new products directly on the shoulders of the sales team. We required that they make a business case (a mini business plan) to show why the addition of the product or service was financially viable. And this is where the value of transparency in our financials was illuminated. When the salespeople could see for themselves the cost of expanding the scope of the business, they were more likely to align themselves with what was best for the company long term.

When a salesperson is part of the ROI process for product development, they realize the product must compete with other projects for company resources, even if there is a strong potential for a good return. They must decide which product will benefit the company

> "They begin to think like entrepreneurs and understand that all opportunities have costs to weigh."

most. They begin to think like entrepreneurs and understand that all opportunities have costs to weigh. For these reasons, among others, I found it vital that the salespeople have full transparency in the cost of goods. It drove them to make better decisions on what to sell, to whom, and at what price.

NO TO NEW BUSINESS

Don't freak out. Of course, you'll want to continuously bring in new business! I'm just warning you that—

- All customers and all business are not of equal value to your company.
- Some accounts will never be profitable.
- Taking on new clients at the wrong time can create serious problems.

Let me explain. When LetterLogic was just a few years old, I participated in a golf tournament where my foursome included Jerry Killough, the founder and CEO of a very successful healthcare software business. Since we were sharing a cart, we talked about everything under the sun—everything but business—and we bonded over our love for our granddaughters. By the end of the day, we were friends for life.

A few months later, Jerry called to see if I was interested in getting his business. That's like asking a six-year-old if they want ice cream. Of course I wanted his business. He had a huge company, and it would be our second-largest customer. What a coup! After some discussion and learning why he was interested in leaving his current vendor, I asked him to send a test file so we could study the data.

Matt, our resident IT guru, reviewed the data. He concluded that their format would not work well in our system, and he could understand why the other vendor was having such a hard time pleasing the customer. While Matt was usually confident in our ability to work with any type of file, he was worried they'd end up disliking us as much as they did our competitor if we took them on. Together, Matt and I decided we had to say no to the opportunity. Yes, we chose to walk away from an account that would have generated millions in annual revenue.

I called Jerry to deliver the news. I told him I'd rather keep him as a friend and golf buddy than have him as an unhappy customer, so I had to respectfully decline the business. I also told him that if his data were ever available in a more compatible format, I'd love to have the chance to work with him.

That did not harm us; it actually solidified our professional relationship. Turns out, Jerry wanted to give us a chance, but he was worried that we really weren't ready yet for his account. Our careful analysis and conscientiousness convinced him we would be good partners after all. Without fanfare, he went about making the changes internally to create our preferred data format. A few months later, he called to tell me that the work was complete and now he'd like to move his business over. We landed one of our biggest customers by saying no.

Firing Your Customers

Sometimes saying no to business means firing customers, and there were a few occasions when we had to sever ties with customers who were not a good fit for us. In most of those cases, we had to take that action because the customer did not appreciate our unique employee-first culture, and that was not an area in which we were willing to compromise.

One occasion comes to mind immediately. After several great years, a customer had a management change, and we had to deal with a new contact. From the get-go, the new person was surly and rude, and he took to berating and hassling his account manager, Carrie Sublett, who happens to be one of the best communicators I know. She is highly intelligent and capable of understanding complex IT issues and explaining them to non-technical people. She is patient, kind, and beautiful inside and out.

Carrie had been dealing with this customer quietly on her own. She didn't tell anyone that he yelled and belittled her. But one of her coworkers overheard him cursing at Carrie and came to me about it. In keeping with our employee-first commitment, my first step was to call and introduce myself to the new client contact. He couldn't have been nicer.

But I was up to date on the facts of his situation before I went into the call, having read the Salesforce records. Even in his email exchanges, he was condescending and contemptuous. Once into the call, I told him I'd been made aware of some of the conversations he'd had with Carrie. I told him I'd read his emails, and I requested that he treat her with the respect she deserved going forward. His first reaction was to exclaim how good she was at her job, and he agreed to try to be more professional. But a leopard doesn't change its spots.

Before long, he was back at it, yelling at Carrie so loudly over the phone that others in the department could hear him. That was it. Without hesitation, I fired this customer. I gave them the required thirty-day written notice of cancellation and asked that they change our primary contact to someone other than this man until the agreement was over.

Carrie told me how much it meant for me to fight for her and to go as far as to fire a profitable customer due to his behavior. She said, "You always say we're like a family, and we *are*. You stood up for me like I was your very own sister. Thank you for not letting him abuse me." It was my pleasure to get rid of that guy. The price of doing business with him was simply too high.

"Opportunities" to Avoid

Admittedly, we all want to grow our companies and, especially in the early years, we say yes to business that isn't a good fit. Here are the most common "opportunities" you will likely encounter, and which I recommend you avoid:

⬡ **Taking business at a loss, just to get your foot in the door.**

I've done it. I've taken on accounts at a loss because I thought they would open doors. Those doors rarely opened. Eventually, I had to either terminate the customer or hugely increase their rate to make continuing with them profitable. The one scenario where taking business at a loss could be feasible is if there is a short conditional trial period, as part of the contractual agreement, with an automatic price escalation thereafter. The "automatic" escalation part is crucial because it's too difficult to go back to the customer sixty days into the relationship and remind them that the pricing is going to increase soon. Just make it easy on yourself and build the price jump into the initial agreement.

⬡ **Doing business with friends and family.**

Something weird happens when you do business with friends and family. The expectations are totally out of whack on both sides. They think they are doing you a favor by "giving" you some business. You think you're doing them a favor by "giving" them a lower rate. A "friends and family" discount typically translates to a loss, which means the customer is unconsciously placed at a lower priority level. The customer soon grows disenchanted and feels unappreciated. See how this works?

I don't care how good the friendship is or if the customer is your identical twin. Human nature is human nature. I would rather not have their business than risk placing my closest relationships in jeopardy. Just say no, and you'll never have to deal with this problem.

 Taking on business that does not fit your business model.

Saying yes to business outside your core strength will not benefit anyone. When you take on non-core strength business, your team will struggle to deliver high-quality goods/services; team morale will suffer because your team takes pride in their work and they know when it's inferior; your customer will be disappointed and disenchanted; and your brand will be damaged. Oh, and you won't make any money! 'Nuff said.

NO TO UNNECESSARY NETWORKING EVENTS

There are 14,001 people who want to take up your time today. Maybe they're hoping you will buy something from them or introduce them to someone, or perhaps you're hoping they'll buy something from you or introduce you to someone else. Choose carefully what you make time for.

Too much networking will kill you. I've heard it described as "death by a million coffees." Your time is your most precious commodity. Every hour

> "Your time is your most precious commodity."

you give up to a networking event is an hour that could be spent on planning and executing business strategy. That doesn't mean that networking doesn't have value. It just means that every networking event needs to serve an agenda—*yours!*

For example, choose a networking group whose attendees are already operating in or near your industry, or where there is an opportunity to expand an established relationship. Better yet, attend networking events where a few of your customers will be in attendance. An introduction to prospective customers from an existing one is a powerful selling strategy.

As an introvert, I shy away from most networking activities. But since most of my customers were members of the Healthcare Financial Management Association (HFMA), the sales team and I made an effort to attend every HFMA event. It was the perfect place to spend time with our clients and let them bring us into their networks. And they did.

NO TO SERVING ON A NONPROFIT BOARD OR COMMITTEE

Don't yell at me. I love volunteer work. It's good for you and your community and the world. And there will be a time for it. But if you're a new entrepreneur, now is not the right time. Right now, the best thing you can do is concentrate on being a good leader and building a strong company. When you do that, you will develop dozens of smart leaders who can then spend time on philanthropic work and volunteerism, multiplying the good work in your community. When the company is running smoothly, *then* you can take on board work. By that point, your experience will be much more valuable to the organization you're serving.

There's another thing: If your company is not running like a Rolex, and you are spending a good chunk of your time sashaying around the community serving on this board and that board, your employees will think you're a fraud. They know that any time you spend on other companies or nonprofits is time away from the "family" to which you already made a commitment. You owe it to them to keep your focus. There will be plenty of time for community work as soon as your ship is in order.

NO TO LUNCHES, MEETINGS, AND LUNCH MEETINGS

If you're doing well, eventually everyone will want time with you. Even if they have good intentions and aren't trying to poach your sales team or wrangle an introduction, you'll start to feel the burden of these seemingly innocuous requests. They come in the form of "Wanna grab a coffee and . . ." Or, "Let's have a quick lunch and . . ." Or, the one I hate most—"I just want to sit and hear how you built your company . . ." This is shorthand flattery for *I want to sell you something and this is a good way to get time with you.* (I might sound jaded, but I'm right!)

The best way to handle endless requests for your invaluable time is to ask for an agenda. I told people my focus was my employees and that time away from them had to be spent on things that would ultimately benefit them. So I asked for an agenda, which forced people to be specific with their meeting goals and enabled me to determine if it was worth my time.[7]

FEARS ABOUT SAYING NO

Saying no is not easy. It causes fear. Maybe you're afraid that—

- You won't get another opportunity.
- You may not close any other business this month, so you'd better say yes to this opportunity.
- The person will get mad and take their business elsewhere.
- If you miss an event, you'll miss the chance to meet so-and-so.
- If you say no to this invitation to serve on this prestigious board, you'll never get asked again.

---

7   My entrepreneur friend Michael Brody-Waite has a brilliant way of dealing with all the people who "just want some time." He sets aside a certain number of hours every month and invites all the people who have asked to meet with him to gather at the same time. He finds they get value from meeting each other in addition to getting time with him. Those meetings allow him to see if he wants or needs more time with an individual one-on-one.

- If you say no to fundraising for this philanthropic organization, people will think badly of you.

- If you say no to a cross-selling opportunity and it really takes off, you'll have missed out on all that money.

FACTS ABOUT SAYING NO

Here are the facts about saying no, according to me—

- You will get even more opportunities when you say no to business that isn't right for you. Customers respect vendors who tell them no and don't try to be all things to everyone.

- You'll close *more* business, and it will be business that's better for you and your company. If you take the crappy or even marginal business, you'll be so distracted by it that you won't have the necessary focus or time for the perfect business opportunity when it comes along. Saying no frees you up to say yes to better things.

- If a customer gets mad at a no and threatens to leave, let them. You don't want petulant customers. You want loyal customers who value honesty and good business practices.

- When you say no to an opportunity to serve in the community, people start to understand that you are busy and your time is valuable. They will respect you and your time *more*, not less. And then they will only ask you to do things that are valuable and important.

- Every time you say no, you give someone else the opportunity to say yes. This is true even of business opportunities. Have a short list of good, solid competitors to whom you can refer business when an opportunity isn't a perfect fit for you. I constantly referred off-focus business to a favorite local competitor, which accomplished two key side benefits. I satisfied the customers' needs by referring them to a good vendor, and I helped another small business grow by referring good business their way.

- People won't like you less when you say no. *They will like you more.* They will understand that you're saying no because you don't have time to do justice to the commitment they're asking for. They'll actually admire you for saying no.

- You aren't missing out by not selling for other companies. Your salespeople aren't vending machines that dole out commodities. They are highly trained professionals. They appreciate it when you value their time and expertise and don't sell it off to the highest bidder.

WAYS TO SAY NO

Don't worry: There are graceful ways to say no so you don't feel like you're burning bridges. First off, remember that "No." is a complete sentence. Don't offer any excuses. If you do, you are boxing yourself into a corner and—eventually and resentfully—you'll end up saying yes. Instead, here are some unyielding ways to say no:

- No, it's not a good fit for me, but thanks for thinking of me.

- No, now is not a good time for me, but please ask me again next year.

- I respect the work your organization is doing, but it isn't something I'm particularly passionate about. However, a friend has an impressive background in this arena and she is actively looking for volunteer work. Please, may I introduce the two of you?

- I'm crazy about the work you're doing, and I look forward to the time when I may be able to devote time to it, but for the foreseeable future, my support will be strictly financial. May I donate on the website or do you prefer I mail a check?

- I'm flattered that you thought of me, but I've just cleared my calendar to spend more time with my grandchildren (on my business, my hobby, my church), etc.

Avoiding long explanations with your no will prevent the asker from modifying their request to try to work around your excuse.

THE YES CRITERIA

Any ask or invitation that comes my way today (as when I led LetterLogic) needs to meet the following criteria before I say yes:

- ☑ It must bring value to me personally, or to the employees, or the company, or the community. In that order. This is not selfish. If you won't benefit in a way that translates into a positive for your family or employees or the community, there is no tangible reason to do it.

- ☑ It must be something I'm personally passionate about. A few years ago, I was invited to join a board for an organization dedicated to land preservation. Though I value their work, support their mission, and frequently donate, my passion is to promote entrepreneurship, so I said no to being on their board.

- ☑ I must have time for it. At this point in my life, anything that I *add* means I have to *subtract* something else. So it must be important enough that when I say yes to it, I'll have no qualms extricating myself from previous commitments. Something has to give.

Say no. Early and often. Practice it every day.

TAKEAWAY BOX:
With every NO, you create more space to say YES to something else, something that will be better for you and your company.

14

Crème de la Crème
Mentors, Coaches, and Your Tribe

"No one who cooks, cooks alone. Even at her most solitary, a cook in the kitchen is surrounded by generations of cooks past, the advice and menus of cooks present, and the wisdom of cookbook writers."

–Laurie Colwin

INGREDIENTS:

SHARED EXPERIENCES.

For several years, my favorite TV commercial was a spot for a swimming pool business. It featured an attractive young woman who spoke to me directly through the television as each summer approached. "It's gonna be hot and you're gonna want a pool!" she declared. And, every year, as spring runs into summer, I think about that commercial and wish I'd started on that pool last year. I figure that if I called today to buy a pool, the hot summer would be over before the pool was ready, and it would just be a waste of money, until the next hot day when I want a cool pool to dive into.

Unless you're in the pool business, you're probably scratching your head and wondering how this is relevant to my business philosophy. (Those of you in the pool business are probably scratching your heads too, but you're grateful I've put in a plug for your business.)

Here's the connection: You're going to run into problems you can't solve. You're going to have big issues that crop up out of nowhere. And you're going to need a pool of experts to help you find a solution. And you need to have them at the ready, to jump in with you whenever you need them, not months later when the crisis is over. Follow me now?

Think about five to ten entrepreneurs you know best. What do they all have in common? Are they stubborn, headstrong, highly driven, seemingly invincible, always right, myopic? In my experience, even the humblest founders have a stubborn streak that makes it difficult for them to see potential pitfalls that are right in front of them. And they need a pool of advisors to keep them in check.

Over the years, I've created my own pool of mentors, coaches, advisors, and a few "tribes" I can call on at a moment's notice. Some are former bosses. One is a paid coach (who is very expensive but worth every penny). Another was so smart I married him. Others are businesspeople I've built relationships with over time who'll take my call no matter how busy they are. And then there's my peer-to-peer entrepreneurial group that is invaluable to me. In addition to all that brainpower, I also had a board of directors and an advisory board. At some point or another, I've needed them all.

It took a village of individuals and organizations and peer groups, and all of them have been absolutely vital to my success. Let me introduce you to a handful of them and share the unique way each of them helped me.

LISA SCHIFFMAN AND EY
(FORMERLY ERNST & YOUNG)

You're likely confused as to why I would name one of the largest professional services firms in the world as a mentor/coach. It all started when I received a phone call from Lisa Schiffman. She has the longest title in the world—"Director, Brand, Marketing and Communications, Americas Growth Markets."

Lisa called me in 2009 to tell me I'd been nominated for the Ernst & Young Entrepreneurial Winning Women™ program, and she set up a time to interview me during the selection process. At that time, LetterLogic was receiving lots of recognition for our fast growth and unusual culture. We'd been enjoying a spate of awards and accolades. So I wasn't entirely surprised when Lisa called to say I was one of a small group of women founders in the United States nominated for the honor that year.

I assumed the award ceremony would be similar to others I was familiar with. They'd host a dinner event, and the nominees would spend a few thousand dollars to buy a table. They'd have a chance to mingle until the winners were announced. It would be fun and exciting, and then it would be over and everyone would go back to work the next day, business as usual.

Boy, was I wrong. EY Entrepreneurial Winning Women is an executive leadership program unlike any other. It was developed by EY to level the playing field for women business owners so they could scale their companies as effectively as their male counterparts. An evergreen program versus a one-time award, it is undeniably a game changer for those selected by an independent judging panel to join each year's class.

EY also hosts an annual invitation-only CEO conference for business leaders, high-growth entrepreneurs, and the ecosystem that fuels them, the Strategic Growth Forum (SGF). The four-day conference of about 2,000 executives is held in Palm Springs, CA, every November. The country's most successful CEOs rub shoulders with hot-shot new entrepreneurs, a smattering of top-notch celebrities (entrepreneurs too), investors, and deal makers who are there to find the next big thing. SGF is a BIG DEAL that culminates in the largest gathering of entrepreneurs in America, the Entrepreneur of the Year® US National Awards gala, a black tie ceremony hosted in recent years by the likes of Seth Meyers. There are typically 11 industry categories with an Entrepreneur of the Year winner in each, and one winner selected from among them as the US national overall award winner.

Previous Entrepreneurs of the Year in the program's 33-year history include Michael Dell (Dell Computers); Herb Kelleher (co-founder of Southwest Airlines); Howard Schultz (Starbucks); Jeff Bezos (Amazon); Sergey Brin and Larry Page (Google); Reid Hoffman and Jeff Weiner (LinkedIn). I told you: It's a big deal.

Do you notice anything unusual about that list of winners, though? Lisa Schiffman had noticed too: Too few women founders were being recognized for their entrepreneurial accomplishments, and none had ever won the US national overall award. Determined to find out why, she ended up learning that women founders simply weren't given the same access to capital, networks, or markets as their male counterparts. Lisa then approached some of EY's leadership (lots of women in that category at EY) and suggested the firm could create a program to help change the status quo. They agreed, and the EY Entrepreneurial Winning Women program was born to give women who are growing scalable companies the know-how, access to networks and private investors, and media attention they needed but often didn't receive.

There I was, the result of Lisa's initiative, selected by EY to be named to their 2009 class of Entrepreneurial Winning Women. To ensure that I and the other winners were prepared for the firestorm of media attention we were about to get, EY invited us to their Times Square Americas headquarters for an all-expense-paid one-and-a-half day orientation and crash course on entrepreneurial success factors. On the agenda was how to: ace a media interview; perfect our "elevator pitch"; work *on* the business instead of *in* it; build boards of advisors; and get the most out of the Strategic Growth Forum, where we would be introduced to a ballroom full of the most successful and powerful women and men in the country. Some of the people in attendance would be eager to invest in our companies and do business with us.

The day before my trip to New York, I learned I needed a major surgery that could not be delayed. The surgery was scheduled just nine days before the big SGF event in Palm Springs. Knowing I wouldn't be able to attend the event, I decided to go to NYC for the preparatory meeting so I could thank Lisa for the honor in person.

Wow! I absolutely was not prepared for the energy, support, and training I received from EY. They spared no expense, extending resources to us that we would never have gotten otherwise. And when they described how this meeting was just to get us prepared to get the most out of an even more impressive SGF experience, I realized I simply could not miss it. The opportunities were too great. My doctor reluctantly gave me the go-ahead, and a few weeks later, just nine days after a major medical event, I was on a plane to California.

I was already a fast fan of EY but they outdid themselves in Palm Springs. When I walked into my hotel room, a brand new, bright-red scooter was waiting for me. EY wanted to make sure I was able to navigate the massive resort post-surgery. That level of consideration and empathy spoke to me.

The Forum itself was beyond anything I could have imagined. I was interviewed by *The New York Times*, *Forbes*, *Success*, *Inc.*, and numerous other media outlets. I got to meet Jane Pauley (and have the photo to prove it!), someone I'd admired for years. And I had a cocktail with Tony Hsieh, CEO of Zappos. Yes, I did. Most important, I became part of the EY Winning Women family, which now includes 10 more classes of women founders in the United States and Canada. The EY teams truly do everything in their power to help us grow our companies and become better leaders.

Fresh from the power of the SGF, I asked my CFO to move our accounting business to EY. A few days later, a few local EY professionals met with us for a half day to discuss our status and needs. I was surprised when they advised us *not* to move our business to them. They said our current vendor was appropriate for our size and needs at that time; a move to EY would only make sense later, when we were larger and our needs more complex. Can you imagine how much more faith and confidence I had in them after that discussion?

Entrepreneurial Winning Women has been a success for everyone associated with it. The program, which is now global, includes more than 500 women founders from 65 countries across the world. Many of my 2009 classmates have grown companies worth hundreds of millions of dollars, and even a few worth *billions*. We all credit EY.

I've only missed a few SGFs since 2009, and every year is better than the last. In 2017, I got to meet one of my heroes, Madeleine Albright. I also met two women entrepreneurs, Fran Dunaway of TomBoyX and Danyel Surrency Jones of PowerHandz. And guess what? I invested in both their companies. We were thrilled to be in attendance at the US Entrepreneur of the Year national awards gala that year, when five of the 11 national industry category winners were women—including one who rose from the 2013 class of Entrepreneurial Winning Women to win the national Technology category and another who, with her business partner, took home the US national overall award!

If Madeleine Albright is right and "there's a special place in hell for women who don't help other women," then I'm sure there's a "special place in heaven" for Lisa Schiffman, Kerrie MacPherson, Katie Johnston, and the invincible team of women and men at EY who stopped talking about leveling the playing field for women and just did it. I love them.

CLARK GABLE (NO, NOT THAT ONE.)

In the mid-1990s, I was working for a waste management company selling site services to construction companies in the Nashville area. Site services included portable toilets, large dumpsters, temporary fencing, storage containers, and even office trailers. My company car was a white Ford F-150 pickup truck.

My on-the-job training came from Ann Johnson, an effervescent blonde who'd drive up to a job site, jump out of her company truck in jeans and cowboy boots, clipboard in hand, and approach the job superintendent. "Let's talk trash!" she'd say. She was a fun, kind, and patient teacher who taught me the basics of the trash business before I was assigned my own territory.

Since my father was a building contractor, I'd grown up around plumbers and carpenters and electricians. I was in my comfort zone on construction sites. If I'd been the type to just do my job and keep my mouth shut, it's likely I'd still be working there. But even then, I had to challenge the status quo, beginning with the paperwork requirements.

The salespeople had to complete and turn in an activity booklet each week that included details about who we'd called on, what we'd talked about, and what we'd sold. Each service came with its own contract and work orders. It seemed to me I was wasting a lot of valuable selling time filling out forms when my time would be best spent *selling*.

I hypothesized that if a salesperson were actually out building a clientele, you'd know it because the sales would start pouring in. And if they weren't, the lack of results would speak for themselves, negating the need to fill out a bunch of papers just to prove you were working. I constantly complained about the paperwork until my supervisor acquiesced, probably just to shut me up.

I was a good sales rep, though, and for the first time ever, I was making enough money to support myself and Whitney. But my independence and grit didn't sit well with my boss. After some time, I was "transferred" to the medical waste division of the company.

The transfer was one of the best things that ever happened to me. It forced me to stretch and learn and grow. And it led me to my first great mentor, the person I'm calling "Clark Gable," and, one of the smartest people I've ever known. Clark was leading the company's medical waste division, but he hadn't been allowed the option of choosing me and hiring me. Instead, I was foisted on him by a company that just didn't know how to deal with me.

The first time I laid eyes on Clark was when he picked me up curbside at the Charlotte, North Carolina, airport as I arrived for training. I was so intimidated. He had been a high-ranking military officer, and he had a very stoic, stern disposition. Nervously, during our first fifteen minutes together, in my typical blurt-it-all-out fashion, I confessed that I was terrified. I was worried about selling to doctors and healthcare executives because I only had a high school education.

I don't remember Clark's exact words, but his response was something along the lines of: "Are you stupid? Because if you are, then I agree with you. But if you aren't, you can learn everything you need to know, and you'll be fine." Of course, I wasn't stupid, I told him. And that was that.

I learned so much from him. He taught me the meaning of a Pyrrhic victory (though he could never quite tame my desire to fight the battle). He corrected my grammar. He taught me basic business math. He taught me to let go of pettiness. He taught me (and had to reinforce a couple times) not to gossip. And he believed in me. His confidence in me made me start believing in myself. His wisdom and life experiences showed me that my world was very small and that I had to expand my boundaries if I wanted to experience my full potential. He pushed me out of my comfort zone, and as a result, I learned to adapt to new situations, which allowed my confidence to grow by leaps and bounds.

When Clark moved on to his next leadership role with another company, he asked me to join him as vice president of sales. The move enabled me to continue to grow and learn from him for a few more years before we both moved on to other industries.

Without hesitation, I will tell you that I would be a different person, leading a much different life, had I not met him.

MARK DEUTSCHMANN

If you ask me who's been my most influential mentor and where I met him, my answer would be Mark Deutschmann—my now-husband—and I got his number off a bathroom wall. For real.

When LetterLogic was about five years old, I spent most of my time selling to hospitals across the country. I was constantly on planes and in rental cars, running from city to city. When I was home on the weekends, I frantically tried to take care of the house and lawn—cutting the grass, cleaning the gutters, you name it.

At the end of one spring day, my by then adult daughter, Whitney, met me at the local pizza joint, Mafiaoza's, for a beer. She tried to convince me to sell the house and move to a condo so I'd have more free time. I reminded her that I'd had my cottage on the market for almost two years and hadn't been able to sell it. Perhaps I should just rent it out and move on?

Halfway through our second beer, Whitney made a quick trip to the ladies' room. When she returned, she insisted I go back to the restroom and "get that guy's number." She was referring to a type of advertisement by Graffiti Indoor Advertising inside the restroom stall that promotes everything from shoe repair services to real estate. There was an ad for some soon-to-be-built condos in the old Kress store building in downtown Nashville. I got the number, called the guy, and made an appointment to see the building.

A few days later, I met Mark Deutschmann for the first time. I took my friend Terry with me. The three of us shook hands on the sidewalk at 5th Avenue North. Carefully, we navigated the dilapidated old building. Mark was professional but very aloof. I didn't for a minute consider him in a romantic light. But Terry did. While I was checking out the potential for a new home, Terry was checking out my realtor. He couldn't stop talking about Mark and how cute he was; specifically, how good he looked in his jeans. I said I hadn't noticed, and I wasn't interested.

However, over the next few days and weeks, I spent more time with my new realtor and began to feel the first tug of attraction. I didn't buy the first property he showed me, but Mark helped me find my new home in an old mid-rise office building that was being converted into condos. I would be the first resident there, and my unit would take about six months to complete.

In the meantime, I asked him to help me sell my house that had been on the market for two years already and whose listing contract had just expired. I explained to him that I thought the house hadn't sold because the price was too low and potential buyers thought there must be something wrong with it. He agreed with me, and we listed the house again at 20 percent higher than it had been a month prior. Six days later, we got a full-price offer. My realtor was getting cuter by the minute.

As we worked through the details of our two real estate transactions, I became more intrigued with Mark as a person. He was always so calm. He exuded a quiet kindness that was very appealing. He was intelligent but humble—a great combination. And, as Terry had noticed early on, he was really cute. I began flirting with him mercilessly, but it was always one-sided. He never even acknowledged I was female. Maddening!

Finally, on closing day, Mark handed me the keys to my new condo, along with a congratulatory card and . . . a suggestion that we go out for a cocktail. We had our first date at Mafiaoza's, the same place where I'd found his number on the back of a bathroom stall. On that date, Mark told me he hadn't responded to my flirting because he didn't think it was ethical to get personally involved with clients. Thank goodness I was no longer his client.

Over the next three years, most of my dates with Mark were dominated by the exchange of business updates. Where he excels on the IQ side of the equation, with an MBA and degrees in marine zoology, international business, and Spanish, my EQ was definitely higher. While I challenged him to know his people better, he challenged me to know the "numbers" of my business better. What was the EBITDA? What was the cost per unit? *The profit per unit?* What was the valuation multiple in my industry? When I closed a new account that added $350,000 per month in business, what did that mean to the valuation of my company? The questions kept on coming!

Mark became my greatest mentor. Not because he coached me or told me what to do, but because he asked questions that I should have been able to answer but couldn't. In so doing, he pushed me to continue learning and expanding my horizons. You'll have to read his book (www.OneMileRadius. com) if you want to hear about our courtship from his vantage point.

Mark and I have learned to lend a listening ear to each other, but to also respect that sometimes, the other person only needs to vent and doesn't want or need advice. If one of us describes an issue we're dealing with, the other will listen and ask if feedback is wanted. If the other offers unwanted advice, the recipient simply says, "thank you"—a subtle way to signal that advice is not wanted. Admittedly, his "thank-you" comes off nicer than mine does, but we've found this to be a good way to draw a line when needed.

ELIZABETH B. CROOK

After Mark and I had been dating for about a year, he suggested I meet with Elizabeth Crook. She's a corporate strategist and executive coach. Mark had found working with her so valuable to his business that he invited her to join his board. I made an appointment with her, hoping she could help me craft a growth strategy.

Early on the morning of our scheduled appointment date, I learned that our CFO had "misappropriated funds." I called Elizabeth to cancel our meeting so I could deal with this emergency situation. When I told her why, she insisted that she was coming anyway and would help me determine the right action to take.

First, Elizabeth is a beautiful woman, elegant and refined, and powerful. She has crystal-blue eyes that see everything. And she has a subtle way of taking charge before you know what has happened to you. So, fifteen minutes after I met her, I spilled my guts and told her everything—how

I'd built the business on a high school education, how my lack of business knowledge led me to hire the CFO (a CPA with an MBA), and how I'd largely turned over the finances of the business to him, with no oversight. I told her I'd just learned we were at least $200,000 in the hole as a result of this bad player I'd fired that morning.

She asked questions. She listened. She took notes. And, two exhausting hours later, she posed an unlikely question: "Did you see *The Wizard of Oz*? Do you know the story of the scarecrow?"

> "A traditional mentor can help you with a few facets of your business, but a paid coach helps you with YOU."

I was a little aggravated at the irrelevance of the question but I answered, "Of course I do." She took a sheet of white paper from the table and rolled it vertically into a long tube. Then, she handed it to me with a flourish and declared: "Here's your diploma. From now on, don't tell anyone you aren't educated. You are one of the smartest CEOs I've ever met, and you're not going to let a slip of paper hold you back."

Thus began my lifelong coaching relationship with Elizabeth. You can access her wisdom when you read her book, *Live Large: The Achiever's Guide to What's Next*.

You're going to need your own Elizabeth. You need someone who sees the forest *and* the trees. You need someone who knows the real you; someone who knows your strengths and weaknesses and can see the blind spots you can't. A traditional mentor can help you with a few facets of your business, but a paid coach helps you with YOU. They help you get out of your own way. They help you set a course and hold you accountable.

THE ONE AND ONLY MICHAEL BURCHAM

Michael Burcham has rock-star status in the entrepreneurial world. I'd heard about him for a few years before I was ever face-to-face with him. We finally met when we were both panelists at a business conference. At that time, Michael had recently launched the Nashville Entrepreneur Center. He'd already created and sold a few successful companies.

Aside from Michael and myself, there were two local venture capital guys on the conference panel. It seemed that I was the outlier: the only female and the only non-MBA. The three guys already knew each other, and as we took our seats on stage, they craned their heads around me to talk to each other. The program began, and I didn't have a chance to meet them.

During the panel discussion, the others talked about which companies they'd invested in and why. I recall talking about my investor, Lucius Burch III, and how he'd honored my unorthodox approach to business. I talked about my belief in the employee-first, empathetic leadership business model.

> "It was the most valuable leadership training I have ever received, and it was a gift."

Afterward, Michael introduced himself and complimented me on the message. He observed that it seemed to really resonate with the audience members. Do you know what that was like for me? Imagine you're a golf novice and one day, quite by accident, Tiger Woods sees you out on the driving range and compliments your swing. That's what it was like for me to be recognized by Michael.

A few weeks later, he gave me a once-in-a-lifetime opportunity. He hand-selected four other entrepreneurs *and me* to spend a few very intense days with him in what I can only describe as a crash course in leadership. I've never asked him why he chose me; I'm only grateful that he did. While he could have charged us tens of thousands of dollars (and we would have paid it), he didn't ask for a dime. Instead, he implored us to open our minds and to learn from each other, to drive each other to greater success, and then, to help other entrepreneurs along the way. It was the most valuable leadership training I have ever received, and it was a gift.

Today, Michael is founder and CEO of another fast-growing healthcare company, and as busy as he is, I know he'll always take the time to help me with any business dilemma or personal challenge. I quote Michael so often that he is the only man my husband is really jealous of. I constantly urge people to read Michael's latest blog posts, so I'll do the same to you: You really must read everything Michael writes! He's brilliant.

THE ENTREPRENEURS' ORGANIZATION (EO)

If you are an entrepreneur, as soon as you qualify to join the Entrepreneurs' Organization (EO), join. I mean it. You simply can't do without it. There are only a few instances in this book (and in person) where I give direct advice. This is one of those times. The membership criterion is simple: You must have minimum annual revenue of $1 million and own 50 percent of your business.

EO is based primarily on peer-to-peer learning. You will meet with a small, dedicated group of six to eight peers (from non-competing industries) for three to four hours each month to help each other grow your businesses. Each group is called a "forum," and everything shared is strictly confidential. Giving advice is forbidden. When a person shares an issue with the group, the other members ask clarifying questions about the situation until all the facts are clearly laid out. Then the members share their own experiences related to that topic. They don't share an experience they read about or heard about: They only share their own.

The topics include anything at all that affects you or your business: It can be your health or the health of a close family member, where to find growth capital, your love life, your employees, your investors, your vendors, when to buy a competitor, when to close a division of your own company. The holistic approach works because outside forces affect your ability to grow and scale your business, and your business can adversely affect your relationships and your health.

EO offers entrepreneurs a much-needed diversity of life and business experiences and perspectives. You need a group of women and men who know your weaknesses, your strengths, and who can check your blind spots for you. Your forum will hold you accountable for your personal and professional goals. They will guide and comfort you through the hard times. They will celebrate with you when you reach your goals. I absolutely believe you'll reach them quicker if you're supported by your own tribe.[8]

It might be springtime in your business. Everything is green and growing and the temperature is quite nice. But eventually, it's going to heat up, and you're going to run into periods of scorching issues, and you're going to want a pool. It's best to start building one now, before you need it.

> ## TAKEAWAY BOX:
> Knowledge and experience from folks who've been where you are can help you avoid the cliffs and pitfalls. And if you end up in a ditch anyway, they'll give you a hand up.

---

8   Similar to EO, Women Presidents' Organization (WPO) is a peer-to-peer professional development organization, but its members are women only and must be the president of a company—and the company must have annual revenues of $1 million or more.

Last Course

DESSERT

15

Piece of Cake
No Downside

"Frequently, I've to come regret things I've said. This is not one of those times."

–Anthony Bourdain

There is no doubt in my mind that the primary ingredient to the success of LetterLogic was its empathy-based, employee-first culture. I believe I've laid out a pretty good argument that *your* business will be more successful if you take better care of your people, and I've given you a commonsense approach to doing so.

I'm guessing that you likely fall into one of three camps that I encounter when I tell my story. The first group is made of those people who get it immediately and have already started making changes in their businesses.

The second group consists of those whose businesses, large or small, are struggling to make ends meet and they just can't see how they can afford to do more for their employees. They're focusing on the terrifying thought of giving away 10 percent of profits—which is very hard to fathom. To them, the thought of even giving raises is out of the question.

And finally, there are those whose businesses are bigger and who think that these strategies will work only for small companies. You're the ones who are thinking, "Bless her heart." (Perhaps the phrase "Bless Your Heart" has positive connotations in other parts of the country, or the world, but in the American South, it's a passive-aggressive phrase that means the speaker either pities the recipient of the blessing or is subtly criticizing that person.)

So, let me start with the latter group. *You are wrong!* It doesn't matter how big your company is. An employee-centric, empathetic culture will make a better company. And you know how I know this? Because there are many great examples of big companies, even public companies, that employ this strategy. The proof is out there.

Just look at the example of Scripps Health. In 2000, this large healthcare system was in trouble. They were awash in debt, and they could not attract or keep good nurses. This presented a huge problem for them because California has a strict patient-to-nurse ratio requirement, and losing nurses meant they were constantly in danger of losing their charter. Amid the turmoil, a new CEO, Chris Van Gorder, took over. At the heart of his strategy was listening to employees and taking better care of them. The results were startling.

First, he stopped the employee attrition. The turnaround in employee satisfaction was so great that *Forbes* has named Scripps a "Best Company to Work For" for several years. But how about their financial situation? Their $150 million turnaround is legendary. And that turnaround enabled them to take on a huge $4 billion expansion.

What about those of you in the second group, who are really struggling with cash flow and profitability—sometimes in danger of not even making payroll? You're thinking:

- I can only pay minimum wage because I'm not even paying myself yet.

- I plan to pay more and have better benefits after . . .

- If I share the financials and other details with my employees, they'll know the business better, and they might leave and compete with me.

- Nashville is different; you just don't know our market here in . . .

You've missed the point.

LetterLogic was not successful in spite of our employee-first, empathetic practices. It was successful solely *because* of them. By attending to the needs of the employees, we enabled them to be all-in when it came to their work—and that resulted in superior products and services.

WHAT WOULD HAPPEN?

Just think about this for a few minutes. Think about your two best employees. What would happen if all your employees were as good, as effective, as those two? How would that affect your productivity? Your bottom line? Or what would happen if your customers were so pleased with your consistently exceptional service that they were willing to pay you 10 percent more than they're paying now? What would *that* do to your bottom line? I absolutely believe that our customers were willing to pay more because they knew they wouldn't get the same level of service from any other vendor.

If you begin now, today, with making just one change to show your people that they matter to you, you'll feel the effects by tomorrow. Maybe it'll be subtle at first. Maybe that person who rarely makes eye contact with you will look up and smile at you tomorrow morning. And you'll smile back. And that connection, that human connection, will begin to build a bond that opens doors to more transformative change.

By the time you start implementing your profit share program, you'll find that your entire team is working together to make your company the best in its class. When you hand out those first profit share checks, the joy of successful collaboration will lift the roof off your building. And when you see how that investment in your people affects your bottom line, I hope you'll reach out to me to share your story.

The positive changes in your employees, the improved workplace culture, and the growing revenue will absolutely convince you that the *status quo sux*. None of this is rocket science, and there's no need to overcomplicate the steps you take to do it. It's about human nature, and a person's desire to be valued and respected. Find the path that works for you, your employees, and your business. And commit to it. Remember, happy employees lead to happy customers who will pay a premium for high-quality products and superior service. And, happy, loyal customers lead to satisfying rewards for your shareholders. No downsides there.

One final thought: No one sets out to be an average entrepreneur. So why settle for the same old business model that likely isn't getting you the results you want? Or that doesn't support your vision and values? Why not be a leader who changes the rules? My goal was to show you there's a different, better way. I hope I've done that.

TAKEAWAY BOX:

Your business will absolutely be more successful if you take better care of your people. Put people first. The profit and peace of mind will follow!

Epilogue

A Fable

A man was leaving the United States for a yearlong assignment and needed someone to take care of his horse while he was away. He did some quick research, scouted out the stable with the best reputation, and scheduled a visit.

When he arrived at the property, he was in awe of the pasture's sheer beauty and lush green grass. The horses that freely roamed the land were gorgeous, their shiny coats gleaming in the sunlight. The stable manager approached him with a friendly welcome and a warm handshake. The man was feeling good about boarding his horse here.

"What are your rates?" he asked.

"$2,000 per month, with a $500 rebate for the manure, which we can sell to local farmers," replied the manager.

This seemed quite expensive to the man, so he decided to check out another option.

The second stable was located just a few miles away but the pastures were not nearly as nice; only patches of green grass here and there. The few horses that boarded there looked okay but not as healthy as the horses at the first location. A farmhand sauntered over to the man with a casual greeting. When the man inquired about the rates for keeping his horse for the next year, the farmhand said the rate was $1,000 a month, with a $200 credit for manure, which he could sell.

Since there was such a wide gap between the two offers, the man decided to visit at least one more facility.

The third facility was rough. The stable was in disrepair. There was little grass anywhere, and the horses that boarded there were scrawny, their coats muddy and matted. No one greeted him, and he had to search around the dilapidated property to find someone to talk with.

Finally, he found the stable owner rocking on his back porch. The man inquired about pricing. "$500 per month," he was told. "What about the manure?" the man asked. "What kind of credit are you offering for the manure?"

The stable owner looked at the man incredulously. "Manure? What manure? If you're only paying $500 a month to feed your horse, there won't be any manure."

The moral of the story: If you don't take care of your people, there won't be shit to sell.

LetterLogic Awards

2004	Future 50 Award	Nashville Area Chamber of Commerce
2005	Future 50 Award	Nashville Area Chamber of Commerce
2006	Future 50 Award	Nashville Area Chamber of Commerce
2007	Future 50 Award	*Inc.* magazine
2007	Future 50 Award	Nashville Area Chamber of Commerce
2007	Top 50 Fastest Growing Female-Led Businesses in North America	Women Presidents' Organization
2007	Inc. 5000	*Inc.* magazine
2008	Women of Influence	Nashville Business Journal
2008	Top 50 Fastest Growing Female-Led Businesses in North America	Women Presidents' Organization
2008	Future 50 Award	Nashville Area Chamber of Commerce
2008	Inc. 5000	*Inc.* magazine

2009	Inc. 5000	*Inc.* magazine
2009	Top 50 Fastest Growing Female-Led Businesses in North America	Women Presidents' Organization and Entrepreneur magazine
2009	Entrepreneurial Winning Women Award	Ernst & Young
2009	Future 50 Hall of Fame	Nashville Area Chamber of Commerce
2010	EY Entrepreneur of the Year	Regional Finalist
2010	The Green Award	Nashville Technology Council
2010	Inc. 5000	*Inc.* magazine
2011	Mary Lehman McLachlan Economic Empowerment Award	Women Presidents' Organization, (international award)
2011	Entrepreneur of the Year	City Paper and the Entrepreneurs' Organization
2011	Best in Business	Nashville Business Journal
2011	Economic Empowerment Award	Tennessee Economic Council on Women
2011	Inc. 5000	*Inc.* magazine

2012	Best Place to Work	Nashville Business Journal
2012	Top 30 Influential Nashville Entrepreneurs	
2012	Inc. 5000	*Inc.* magazine
2012	Innovation Award: Mayor's Workplace Challenge	Mayor Karl Dean
2013	Market Mover, NEXT Awards	Nashville Area Chamber of Commerce
2013	Business with Purpose Award	Lipscomb University
2013	Most Powerful Woman	Nashville Post
2013	Mayor's Workplace Challenge, Gold: Greening	Mayor Karl Dean
2013	Mayor's Workplace Challenge, Gold: Healthy Living	Mayor Karl Dean
2013	Mayor's Workplace Challenge, Gold: Community Involvement	Mayor Karl Dean
2013	Inc. 5000	*Inc.* magazine
2013	Best in Business Award	Nashville Business Journal

2014	Women in Business	Nashville Lifestyles
2014	Inc. 5000	*Inc.* magazine
2015	Entrepreneur of the Year	NEXT Awards, Nashville Area Chamber of Commerce
2015	Inc. 5000	*Inc.* magazine
2016	Inc. 5000	*Inc.* magazine
2016	White House Champion of Change	President Barack Obama

About the Author

SHERRY STEWART DEUTSCHMANN is a serial entrepreneur and angel investor. Her first venture was LetterLogic, Inc., a company she founded in her basement and grew to $40 million before selling it in 2016. LetterLogic was named an Inc. 5000 company (fastest-growing privately held businesses in the United States) for ten consecutive years.

Sherry attributes the success of LetterLogic to its unique culture in which the needs of the employees came before those of the customer or shareholder. That culture led Sherry to be recognized by EY as one of their 2009 Entrepreneurial Winning Women. LetterLogic was featured in *The New York Times*, *Forbes* magazine, *Inc.*, and *Fast Company*. Sherry was honored by President Barack Obama as a White House Champion of Change in 2016.

Sherry's passion is helping women-owned businesses get better access to networks, capital, and markets, and in 2015, she was appointed to the National Women's Business Council, a small group of women who advise Congress, the Small Business Administration, and the president on issues related to entrepreneurship for women.

Since selling LetterLogic, Sherry has become an angel investor, specifically investing in women-owned and women-centric businesses. In the fall of 2019, she founded BrainTrust, a company dedicated to helping women entrepreneurs grow their businesses to the pivotal $1 million-in-annual-revenue mark.

Sherry is married to Mark Deutschmann, a real estate developer in Nashville, Tennessee, and is mother to Whitney, stepmother to Chelsea, and grandmother to Nikko and Reagan.